ONE
at a
Time

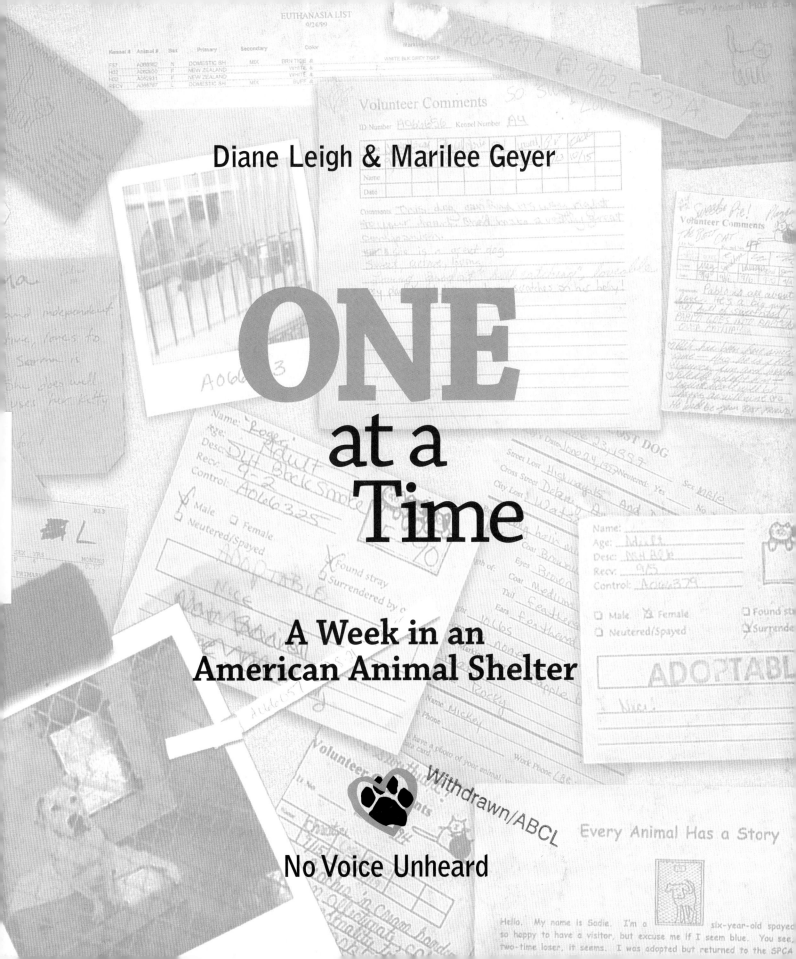

Diane Leigh & Marilee Geyer

ONE
at a
Time

A Week in an American Animal Shelter

No Voice Unheard

Every Animal Has a Story

ISBN: 0-9728387-0-8
Library of Congress Control Number: 2003104016
First Edition 2003

Quotation Credits:

> page 137, *A Language Older Than Words* by Derrick Jensen,
> New York: Context Books, 2000

> page 137, "Broken Contracts" by Kenneth White, in *The Animal's Voice Magazine*,
> Volume 3, Number 2, March/April 1990

> page 138, "Coming to Grips with Cruelty" by William Kunstler, in *Mainstream*,
> The Animal Protection Institute, Volume 24, Number 4, Winter 1993

> page 139, "Culturally Sensitive Cruelty: Politically Correct Animal Suffering" by
> Eric Mills of Action for Animals, in *Country Connections*, Earth Alert,
> January/February 1999

> page 139, *The Outermost House* by Henry Beston, New York: Doubleday, 1928

Design and production by Prism Photographics, Inc., Santa Cruz, CA

Printed in Singapore

Quantity discounts for purchase of this book are available to shelters, rescue groups, and educational organizations, as well as to individuals wishing to give copies of the book as gifts or donations. Photos from the book are also available for purchase. For details contact:

**No Voice Unheard
P.O. Box 4171
Santa Cruz, CA 95063**

www.NoVoiceUnheard.org

This book is made possible in part through a generous grant from PETsMART Charities.

> *PETsMART Charities is a non-profit organization with a vision of a lifelong loving home for every pet. To improve the quality of life for all companion animals, PETsMART Charities creates and supports programs that save the lives of homeless pets, and promote healthy relationships between people and pets. Since 1994, PETsMART Charities has donated more than $24 million to animal welfare programs and, through its in-store adoption programs, saved the lives of more than 1.5 million once homeless pets. For more information about PETsMART Charities call 1-800-423-PETS (7387) or visit www.petsmartcharities.com.*

A list of our other generous donors and supporters is located on the last page of this book.

Contents

This book is dedicated to the animals whose stories are told
within these pages, and to homeless animals everywhere.

May they forgive us . . .

. . . and may we be worthy of that forgiveness
by giving them the only fitting tribute:
to stop the killing.

Remembering Larry

The sleeping dog in the photo opposite this page was named Larry. Actually, we don't know what his name was, but we called him Larry. He came from an animal shelter in the Silicon Valley area of California, a shelter where well over half of the 30,000 dogs and cats handled that year were euthanized.

He was found, alone and on his own, without the benefit of an ID tag which would have provided the critical information to get him back home. Lacking that information, Larry was held as a stray for seventy-two hours and then became available for adoption. He ended up spending twenty-four days in the shelter.

By all rights, he should not have been one of the smaller group of animals who left the shelter alive. Every animal who enters a shelter plays a game in which the odds are stacked against them: too many homeless animals competing for the adoptive homes available. It is impossible for them all to win; those who lose, lose their lives.

In this deadly gamble, Larry had many strikes against him. He was very old, gray fur woven throughout his golden coat, his head almost completely white. His eyes were clouded with cataracts. What teeth he had left were worn down to nubs. He would almost certainly need more veterinary services, special care, and attention than a younger dog.

He did not do well in the shelter kennel. A sensitive dog who thrived on routine and habit, as we later came to know, Larry was traumatized by the unfamiliar surroundings, the noise, and being handled by strangers. He grew increasingly withdrawn and depressed as the days turned to weeks. Next to the other pens full of outgoing, exuberant dogs, his chances for adoption diminished even further.

Throughout those days and weeks, for some reason, the people with whom he lived and from whom he had become separated did not come for him. They did not look for him, perhaps, or they did not look long enough or they did not look hard enough. For whatever reason, no one came for him, and as a result, his life was at risk.

He would have been put to death, held and comforted by one of the caring strangers who worked at the shelter, but for an unlikely stroke of luck that saved him. The shelter manager, whose job it is to decide which animals will be put to death each day, was touched by him and could not face condemning him. Day after day she avoided "dispositioning" him, until his stay stretched far beyond the time the shelter was able to give the vast majority of animals. Finally, she called a rescue group who focus on special needs animals – animals with severe disadvantages in competing in the game of adoption roulette – and asked the group to take custody of Larry and try to find him a new home. That home turned out to be mine.

Larry's story is unusual only in its happy ending. Virtually every community in the United States is serviced by an animal shelter of some kind. The job assigned to these facilities by their communities – the job of the animal sheltering "system" in this country – is to take in lost and stray animals, accept animals surrendered by their "owners," adopt out as many as possible to new and, hopefully, permanent homes, and to "humanely euthanize" the rest.

Eight to ten million animals pass through these facilities each year. They have about a fifty percent chance of getting out alive. Four to six million of them will be euthanized – around a half-million a month nationwide, 575 each hour, one every six and a half seconds. Euthanasia in animal shelters is the leading cause of death of healthy dogs and cats.

There are probably as many ways to quantify this appalling tragedy as there are animals caught in it. And ironically, the more we try to quantify it, the more incomprehensible it becomes. It is almost impossible to imagine millions upon millions of individual animals being received across animal shelter counters, each creating a trail of administrative paperwork, each being examined and vaccinated, kenneled, fed, bathed, walked and played with. It is even more impossible to picture the millions who are put to death.

In fact, the only way to understand the tragedy is to see, to know, that it happens to one animal at a time. One precious dog, one special cat, each with his own individual story, his own unique history, his own sacred spirit and his own uncertain fate. One by one, until there are millions.

This book is about those individuals. It is a testament to the faces we will never see and cannot imagine, because there are too many. It is a way to help us understand that the statistics are more than mere numbers: they are real lives, and they are utterly and completely at our mercy.

Larry lived happily with us for the remaining three years of his life. After a weeks-long period during which he clearly and painfully grieved the loss of his previous family, he finally accepted us as his new one. He learned to be comfortable in our home, adapted to our daily routines, created his own new habits. He played and ran, and slept peacefully. In an attempt to make up for a life-change he should never have had to endure, we gave him the best of everything, made every one of his days as satisfying and happy as we could. We loved him deeply and he returned that love a thousand-fold. When finally he left this world, he did so at a very old age, at home, held, comforted and surrounded by people he knew... as it should be for all companion animals.

In my own heart he was a symbol of all of his brothers and sisters who play the game of chance in our animal shelters, and who play with their very lives at stake. Although Larry beat the odds and won, I could never look into his eyes without thinking of those who lost.

This book is for Larry. And for all the unseen "Larrys", canine or feline, in animal shelters across America, who are forced to play the game.

TELLING THEIR STORIES

The photos in this book were taken during a one week period in a typical American animal shelter in northern California. Each animal's story, as told in these pages, is completely real and truthful. There are no "composite" characters or events; all facts are taken from actual shelter records; every conversation was witnessed by the authors as it occurred. The overall story of what happens to animals in animal shelters in this country is also real.

When we arrived at the shelter on Monday, the kennels were already nearly full, as they almost always are, with 238 animals being cared for. The shelter is open on Mondays for emergencies only, so just five new animals were added that day; all were lost animals brought in from the streets. But on Tuesday morning, when the shelter opened to the public, there was a line of people waiting at the door to surrender their animals, and still more animals arrived as strays. Thirty-five were added to the shelter population that day. During the rest of the week, every day, more animals arrived – another 125 by week's end on Sunday.

For this book we chose, from those who were at the shelter during that week, a random selection of animals to photograph and write about. We met each of them, spent time with them, got to know them. We learned about the circumstances that caused them to be in the shelter, and we followed their stories and waited to see what would happen to them.

There was little to tell us what each animal's fate would be. Stray dogs, whose gleaming coats, trimmed nails, and friendly personalities seemed to indicate that they were well cared for in loving homes, were inexplicably never claimed by their families. Litters of kittens who were utterly irresistible, and who we were sure would be adopted in an instant, were competing with scores of other irresistible kittens – many did not get homes. Funny-looking, unkempt dogs caught the hearts of visitors and did get adopted. There were some obvious exceptions: aggressive dogs and feral cats, for instance, are almost always doomed from the minute they enter a shelter. But for the most part, every animal seemed to us to be at the unpredictable and ominous whim of chance. And the truth is, they were.

At the end of our week, many of the animals we photographed remained at the shelter, and we followed each of their stories until its conclusion. Eventually, each and every animal left the shelter in one way or another. Some of the lost animals were reunited with their relieved families, some lucky animals were joyfully adopted into new homes, and some were euthanized. Our hearts rose or fell, rejoiced or broke, with each happy or tragic ending. Each of the animals became precious to us. Each one, we knew, was gifted with his or her own unique spark of life and spirit. All of them deserved so much more than to be there, fighting for a chance at a safe and happy life.

Not only are the individual stories told in this book absolutely true, but the picture they paint of this shelter is also true. For instance, the proportions of lost animals entering the shelter, versus those willingly given up by their guardians, is reflected accordingly in the numbers of such stories in this book. The ratio of puppies and kittens to adults animals is also accurately reflected by these stories. The number of stories with happy endings, compared to the opposite, is about the same at the shelter as in this book. And though the total numbers of animals or particular mix of circumstances may be different at the shelter in your community, you can be assured that the overall picture is very similar, and that the animals in your shelter have stories quite like the ones in this book.

There is one exception. While this book contains stories of only dogs and cats – and in fact dogs and cats do comprise the vast majority of homeless animals in this country – it bears saying that animal shelters also handle an amazing array of other species whom humans turn into "pets": rodents, reptiles, birds, exotics, farm, and wild animals. Like dogs and cats, and for many of the same reasons, they also become homeless and face the same uncertain fate in shelters.

We have included in every animal's story the "control number" assigned to him by the shelter. The control number matches the animal with the administrative paperwork and records created for him when he entered the shelter. Many people find it offensive and denigrating to label a living being with a number. We agree, but in an institution that processes millions of living beings, numbers are needed to track them within the system. Further, many of the animals caught in this system are completely anonymous, their control number the last thing identifying them, the last, sad way of distinguishing them as an individual amongst the millions of others. We include the control numbers here as a reflection of these realities.

Where we could, we have also included each animal's name. In some cases, we were able to learn the animal's real name – when a guardian gave up the animal and told the shelter the name, or when a lost animal was claimed by his family. But in many cases, we did not know what the animals' names were before they entered the shelter. Some of them were given names by shelter staff or by adopters, which are the names you will see here, and some did not receive a name at all.

As to terminology, there is some controversy over the term "pet owner" as a way to describe those people who live with animal companions. Many believe the word "owner" relegates dogs and cats to the status of property, of *things*. Although animals actually *are* property in the eyes of the law, the term and the concept certainly do not do justice to the companions who share our homes and our lives with us. Recognizing that our language imparts a powerful message about the nature of our relationship with animals, we have chosen in this book to replace the use of "pet owner" with "guardian" – a term more reflective of an attitude of protection and care rather than ownership or possession, and of stewardship rather than dominance of these beings.

One final note on terminology: in some parts of this book, the male pronoun is used. Know that this was done solely in the interests of readability and that no slight to the female gender is intended.

When reading this book and the stories of these animals it will be helpful to understand some aspects of the larger context of the animal sheltering system in this country.

Many people think that all animal shelters in the United States are somehow affiliated with each other, part of some national structure or "chain" operating under an umbrella organization from which they receive funding. This is not true. Local animal shelters are independent facilities with no national "parent" organization. There also is no official terminology defining these facilities. "Animal shelter," "SPCA," "humane society," or "the pound" are all often interchangeably used to refer to shelters.

In general, shelters are run by city or county governments or by independent non-profit organizations. There are some exceptions. Especially in small or rural communities, shelters may be run by individuals, veterinarians, the police department, or animal dealers. (Dealers may sell unwanted animals for research and experimentation. Some animal shelters also do this and in some states, laws called "pound seizure" *require* that unwanted animals be made available for research.)

A large number of shelters in this country are run by non-profit organizations who are hired under contract by their city or county to operate an animal shelter. They may also be hired to provide animal control services such as enforcement of animal related laws, capturing and transporting lost, abandoned, or injured animals from the streets to the shelter, and investigating cases of cruelty or neglect. In contract arrangements, the municipalities most often do not pay for veterinary care, or educational, volunteer or even adoption programs, and so shelters rely on donations to fund these life-saving activities. In many municipalities, the amount the shelter is paid does not even cover the costs of the services being contracted for and donations may make up that difference as well.

One basic attribute of shelters is how each deals with the most fundamental and challenging dynamic of the homeless animal problem: the numbers of animals. Some shelters accept all animals brought to them; when their cages are full, and after exhausting other options, they resort to euthanasia to make room for the new animals who will inevitably soon arrive. Other shelters do not euthanize when their cages become full, and instead stop accepting new animals. They may refer to themselves as "no kill" shelters (although they may still euthanize animals who are incurably ill or injured or who have severe behavior problems).

Most shelters in this country, including municipal shelters and non-profits operating under municipal contract, are of the type that accept all animals brought to them. And, in fact, virtually every community in the country has a shelter performing euthanasia to create cage space, as the current magnitude of the problem dictates that "no kill" shelters could not possibly accommodate the volume of homeless animals

that would arrive at their doorstep.

We tell you this not to defend euthanasia as a means of handling the homeless animal problem, nor to diminish the work that "no kill" shelters do to help homeless animals. But often the public, the media, donors, volunteers, and even shelter workers themselves get caught up in questions focusing on which shelter performs euthanasia and which shelter is "no kill," while the most critical point is lost: there can be no victory declared if any shelter in the community euthanizes just to keep up with the flow of unwanted animals. Shelters of both types would obviously agree: for the animals, the salient question is not whether an individual shelter is "no kill," but whether the entire *community* is "no kill."

The shelter in this book is run by a non-profit organization providing, under contract, animal control and sheltering services to several nearby cities and its surrounding county. The shelter's contract requires that it accept all animals brought to it. Much of what happens in the stories you will read – the dynamics of limited cage space and decisions about animals' fates – is predicated on that requirement, as it is in most shelters.

Although the shelter in this book is quite typical, animal shelters in this country do vary widely. There are communities that have multi-million dollar shelter and educational facilities, and communities with shelters that literally have no running water, heat, or protection from the elements. Not all shelters are staffed by people who care about animals. Intake procedures vary, from simply logging an animal in and putting him in a kennel, to giving him a full medical evaluation and behavioral assessment. Many shelters vaccinate incoming animals against common diseases; some do not. There are shelters with modern, fully-equipped veterinary clinics, and shelters that provide no veterinary care at all. There are shelters that have no facilities for, and simply do not handle, cats. There are shelters with no foster care programs like the ones you will read about, and even some with no adoption programs.

Shelters also vary in how they classify animals. Almost all shelters label animals as "adoptable," i.e., able to be placed in a new home, or "unadoptable," but the criteria for those labels are not consistent. Animals with treatable illnesses, correctable behavior problems, those who are very young or who are older, or those of particular breeds may be labeled "adoptable" or "unadoptable" depending on the shelter they are in. Many shelters use these ambiguous classifications to calculate their statistics. For instance, excluding "unadoptable" animals from the totals used to determine adoption and euthanasia rates makes it nearly impossible to make meaningful interpretations of the statistics or to draw valid comparisons between shelters.

Whatever the varying administrative structures, physical conditions, procedures, and terminology used by animal shelters, what remains consistent throughout are the *animals*. Their lives, their stories and their fates, are the common thread and the truly important thing on which to focus.

It is important to us to show respect to the animals in this book, and homeless animals everywhere, by telling the complete and *full* truth. We feel that it dishonors the animals and what they go through, to tell only the stories with happy endings and exclude the animals whose fates are hard for us to face. As you can easily guess, this means that some of these stories will be sad, some hard to read. Some will break your heart, as they did ours. Writing these stories and reading them is a profound act of "bearing witness," but also, we firmly believe that the truth cannot be *changed* until it can be *seen*. And so we have undertaken to show it here.

But here is the other part of the truth we want to tell you: this tragedy *can* be changed. Remember this as you read, hold *this* truth in your mind. This tragedy is not like others of our time – some far-off crisis over which we feel we have no control, or some issue decided by politicians and lobbyists and moneyed corporations over whom we have no influence. There is no one "in charge" here; we do not have to wait for someone else to "do something."

No, the solutions to the homeless animal problem are in *our* hands. In fact, they are in no one else's – it comes down to each of us. It is us, out here beyond the shelter walls, in our communities, in our everyday lives, in the choices we make and the actions we take, who can end this tragedy. These stories will show you how.

One of our favorite fables is the story about a group of friends having a picnic on a riverbank. They hear the sound of crying and look up, shocked to see a baby floating helplessly in the river. They immediately dive in to rescue the baby, and to their horror, see another baby floating toward them. They rush to save that baby, but no sooner is that one pulled to safety than they see another. And still more appear; the river is full of them. Again and again the people dive into the river, trying to save the seemingly endless flow of drowning babies.

One of the people gets out of the river and begins running upstream. "Where are you going?" his friends shout. "I'm going to find out who's throwing babies in the river and make them stop!" he yells back, as he heads upstream.

The homeless animal problem is a lot like that. Animal shelters and rescue groups try hard to save the homeless animals in the river. But that will never *solve* the problem. Real, lasting solutions to the homeless animal problem involve stopping them from being thrown in the river in the first place.

Remember as you read, *we* are the key to both. There are so many ways that each of us can help. *We* can save the life of one of the "river babies," by adopting our next companion animal from a shelter. And as importantly, *we* can be the ones to keep the babies out of the river. We can keep our animals safely confined and always wearing identification, to prevent them from becoming lost. We can spay and neuter our animals so they do not contribute to companion animal overpopulation. We can make sure we are ready for the commitment before we get a companion, and when we do, we can ensure that commitment lasts a lifetime. We can demonstrate respectful, loving and responsible companion animal care so that others may learn from our example and want to do the same.

These actions may seem basic, even simple, and in many ways, they are. But they are also profound actions that honor our animals' love and companionship, acknowledging their intrinsic value and showing respect for them as living beings. And, they are the actions that, *one at a time,* begin to bring an end to the homeless animal tragedy, and they are within *our* power.

Ultimately, this is the reason we have written this book and chosen to tell the full – and often difficult – truth: so that good-hearted, caring people can learn and gain a deeper understanding of their ability to affect this tragedy and solve this problem. So that they will be able to recognize and use the tools already available to them to help create change. So that compassionate people everywhere come to understand it is in their power to reject the "business as usual" euthanasia of millions of companion animals every year. So that they can begin to build communities that treat our animal friends with love and respect.

We hope you are one of those people.

We were not able to include in this book all of the animals we saw and met during the week we spent at the shelter — there were too many.

Nonetheless, we remember and wish to honor each and every one of them. A complete list of the animals who passed through the shelter during that week can be found in the last pages of this book.

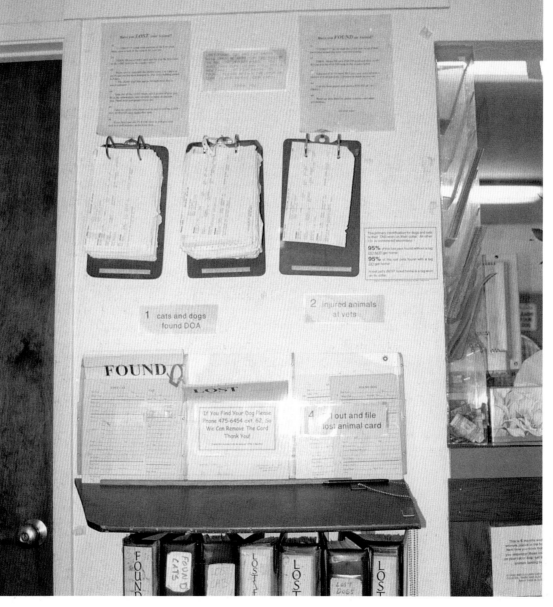

Chapter 1

LOST

It's a dangerous world out there, and everyday, in cities across the nation, dogs and cats by the thousands end up on the streets. Statistics indicate that an animal is lost every thirty seconds and at some point during their lives, one of five companion animals will become lost.

Some of them are dogs and cats who are usually safely confined at home but somehow slip out unnoticed through an open door or an unlatched gate. Many are animals who are routinely allowed to roam on their own, or who are not confined at all.

There are also exceptional circumstances. Fireworks displays are notoriously terrifying to animals, and in their desperate efforts to escape the noise they can, and do, break through windows and screens and end up miles from home. Earthquakes, floods, and other natural disasters result in large numbers of animals becoming lost. In the chaotic aftermath of a car accident, house fire, or other emergency, an animal may flee the scene in confusion and fear.

What happens to these various stray animals is a matter of chance. If they are lucky, they happen across sympathetic people who help them, but many of them will not be that fortunate. Tens of thousands of animals are hit by cars, their bodies picked up by animal control officers and logged in shelter records as "dead on arrival." Others are subject to starvation, injury or abuse. Wandering domestic animals are sometimes killed by wild animals like coyotes and raccoons, even in relatively urban areas. And, in horrifying cases which are not as rare as we'd like to believe, stray animals are picked up by "bunchers," who sell them to animal dealers, who in turn resell the animals to laboratories for use in experimentation.

Some lost animals do make it back home. The critical yet simple key to this happy ending is some form of identification. The most basic and well-known is an ID tag displaying the information needed to get a lost animal home: a phone number, address, guardian's name. Tags come in all shapes, colors, and sizes: tags that hang from collars and others that slide over and lay flat against the collar, plastic and metal tags which are custom-engraved, handwritten laminated paper tags, simple round tags and cute colored tags in the shapes of bones or made of elegant shiny brass. There are even collars which can have a phone number woven into them. With so many varieties available at pet supply stores, veterinary offices and shelters, this basic protection can be a fashion statement as well.

Microchip identification is becoming more common. A small computer chip, the size of a grain of rice and programmed with a number registered to the animal's guardian, is injected just under the animal's skin between the shoulder blades. Many shelters are equipped with scanners that read the information on the chip when passed over the animal's body.

Another method of identification is to tattoo a code number on a dog or cat's inner thigh; the number is registered with a service that maintains contact information for the animal's guardian. This identification has the added advantage of protecting a lost animal from ending up in a research laboratory, as the facilities are reluctant to purchase tattooed animals from animal dealers.

Unfortunately, all forms of identification have disadvantages. Collars and tags can come off or be removed. A microchip requires that an animal be in a shelter or veterinarian's office to scan the information on the chip. And while a tattoo might seem to be the most permanent and therefore most reliable form of identification, it can be difficult to trace and tattoo registries have been known to go out of business, leaving their code numbers useless. Some people tattoo their animal with a driver's license or social security number, but these numbers are not public information and therefore not easily accessible to a person who finds a lost animal.

Experts agree that the safest and most reliable identification is provided by a combination of an ID tag, which is visible and easily usable, and a microchip, which is permanent.

If lost animals are wearing identification tags, it is a simple matter for the people who find them to contact their families. There are other ways for guardians to increase the chance of being reunited with their lost animals: placing ads in the local newspaper listing them as lost, posting flyers around the neighborhood advertising their missing companion, going house to house asking if anyone has seen the animal, using the lost and found listings maintained by many animal shelters and even searching listings on the internet. The key is to utilize as many ways as possible of reaching out and searching for a lost animal.

Animals who are not found by their families and who are lucky enough to survive the dangers of the streets may end up as "strays" in animal shelters, either brought there by concerned citizens or picked up by animal control officers.

When a lost animal enters the shelter, he is subject to a "stray hold" – a designated number of days intended to give his family time to find him at the shelter and claim him. The length of the stray hold period varies depending on state and local laws, usually around three days. If his family finds him at the shelter and claims him, they may be charged an "impound" or "redemption" fee to cover the costs of housing, feeding, and caring for him. Depending on the laws in their community, they

may also be given a citation.

Nationally, however, only 16% of lost dogs and 2% of lost cats are claimed from shelters by their guardians. When a lost animal is not claimed by the time the stray hold expires, he becomes the legal property of the shelter and can be made available for adoption to a new home. He may or may not get one – it is a simple fact that there are more animals vying for homes than there are people coming to shelters to adopt them. Thus, many of the dogs and cats who enter the sheltering system as strays end up part of the euthanasia of massive numbers of homeless animals in this country.

In many areas of the country, especially in warmer climates, a significant portion of the stray animal problem is comprised of feral cats. Feral cats are offspring of cats who were once companions and members of human families: lost cats who were never reunited with their guardians, and cats who were intentionally abandoned or left behind. They live in family groups called "colonies" ranging in size from just a few to dozens to as many as 200. The colonies grow quickly as generation after generation of kittens are born – a female cat can have as many as three litters of kittens each year. If these kittens never have human contact, they grow up fearful of humans, seeming more like wild animals than the companion cats we are familiar with.

Feral cats exist on the fringe of human society, in the shadows, avoiding human contact, scrambling just to stay alive. They live in vacant lots, abandoned buildings, alleys, city parks and college campuses – anywhere there is a ready food source. They scavenge from dumpsters and garbage, and prey upon rats and rodents who are also attracted to these food sources. Many feral cats survive on handouts from kindhearted people whose compassion will not allow these creatures to starve.

It is estimated that there are between thirty and sixty million feral cats living in this country.

They are often considered nothing more than nuisances to the human community in which they live, causing problems with their scavenging, and their territorial behavior such as spraying, fighting, and yowling during mating season. Conflicting and inaccurate information about their hunting of songbirds and wildlife makes them even more unwelcome.

Because of their seeming independence, many people mistakenly believe that cats are capable of surviving and thriving on their own. The life of a feral cat, or any cat who has no human guardian to care for him, is testament otherwise. They are subject to disease, parasites, malnutrition and starvation. Half the feral kittens born do not survive. The average life span of a feral cat is just three to five years, compared to fifteen or more years for an indoor companion cat.

The standard method of dealing with feral cats has been, and mostly still is, to attempt to eradicate the colonies – to trap the cats and euthanize them. It's seldom effective, as it requires that every last cat in the colony be killed, for as long as one female is left, the colony will be quickly repopulated. And, other abandoned and feral cats in the area will move in to fill the gap and breed to the capacity of the territory.

During the last decade, a new alternative has emerged, developed by organizations working to protect and advocate for feral cats, and to find ways to allow them to live safer, healthier lives. Rather than trying to eradicate the colonies, their approach is to comprehensively manage them, with a dedicated caretaker accepting long-term responsibility for a colony. The caretaker provides daily food and water, shelter from inclement weather, and knows and monitors the individual members of the colony.

At the core of the managed colony approach is the concept of "trap – neuter – return." Colony caretakers work to trap each of the cats and transport them to a veterinary clinic where the animals are vaccinated, spayed or neutered, and marked with an "eartip" – a small notch in one ear that visually identifies the animal as sterilized. The cats are then returned to the colony, where the caretaker continues to provide support.

Although the life of a feral cat is never easy, the goal of the managed colony approach is to improve the cats' overall health and comfort, reduce their suffering, and give them a place to live out their lives in relative peace.

The ultimate goal, of course, is to not have feral cats, by preventing the actions that "seed" colonies in the first place – abandoning cats to fend for themselves, or allowing them to roam free and become lost. Domesticated cats are not meant to live this way. They won't survive long, or live well, on their own. For their true health and safety, and for their happiness, cats need to live as cherished, protected and cared for companions in loving human families.

Mostly, the stray animal problem, and resulting euthanasia of so many of these animals, is one facet of the homeless animal problem that could be easily solved with simple efforts: ensuring our companion animals are always safely confined and wearing current identification at all times, always knowing where they are and beginning to look for them the minute it is realized they might be missing, then continuing to look for them, using all means possible, until they are found. Simple efforts indeed, but efforts that do nothing less than recognize our companion animals' dependence upon us, that put our responsibility for them into action, and that acknowledge them as friends and valued members of our families.

Mocha

During the week the photos in this book were taken, Mocha was the *only* stray cat – among nearly 150 who passed through the shelter – who was wearing identification. Sadly, many people don't understand the critical importance of keeping some form of identification on their companions. While it is a more commonly accepted practice to put ID tags on dogs, far fewer people identify their cats. This results in tragedy for millions of lost cats every year, an issue about which shelters try desperately to educate their communities.

Unfortunately, the kind of identification Mocha wore was not foolproof – a hollow, two-piece "barrel" that screws together to hold a tiny slip of paper on which contact information is written. These clever devices are notorious for failing and as expected, the bottom half of Mocha's barrel was missing along with the life-saving information that had been inside it. In a shelter, there are few things more heartbreaking than taking in one of the very rare cats who are actually wearing identification and then finding it is useless.

Mocha's family knew the importance of putting identification on her. Luckily, they also knew to look for her at the shelter; without that effort, they would never have seen her again. Of the lost cats taken in by the shelter, Mocha was a rare exception: she was one of only a handful who were reunited with their families.

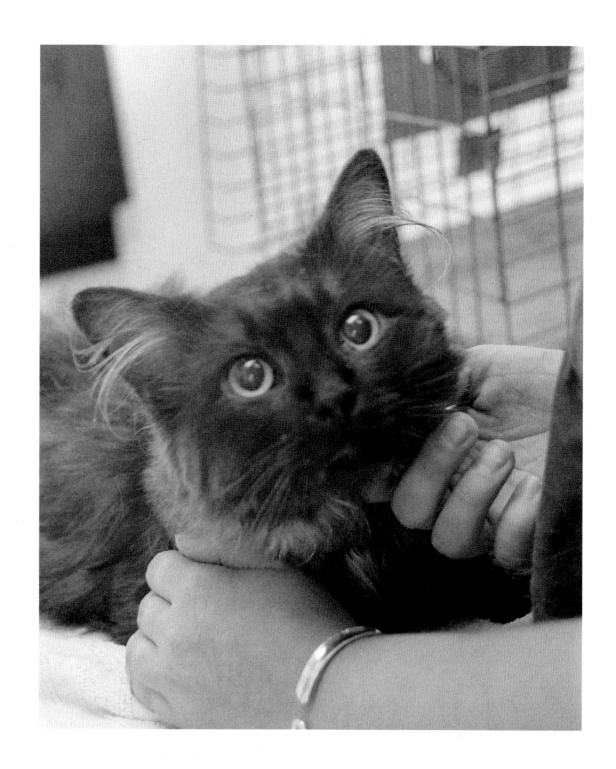

Roger

Roger, as the shelter workers named him, was a gorgeous smoky-black adult cat with large green eyes that seemed to gaze right into you. He was a basic, everyday stray cat. In animal shelters across the country, there are millions of cats with stories just like his.

The lost animal problem is particularly acute for felines. Their reclaim rate is shockingly low. Less than 2% of the stray cats brought to shelters are ever reunited with their guardians. This is due, in large part, to the generally-accepted attitude that cats are independent "free spirits" who need to wander, that they are not quite domesticated and quite capable of taking care of themselves. While it might be an enchanting idea for pseudo-wild animals to be roaming free in our midst, in practice it proves deadly to cats.

The safest, longest lives are enjoyed by indoor cats, who can have satisfying indoor lives, especially when enriched with the delights of toys, cat trees and scratching posts, sunny window seats, cat grass and treats, and playing with their families. Some guardians let their cats safely enjoy the outside, supervised on tethers or leashes, or in outdoor enclosures built specially for them. Outdoor and indoor-outdoor cats have significantly shorter life spans than indoor-only cats, as they are subject to the tremendous risks of vehicles, predators, diseases, injuries, poisons, potential abuse and, like Roger, becoming lost.

People almost universally assume that a missing cat will return on his own. They may not even notice that he is missing right away, and by the time they begin to look for him, he could have been in the shelter and already gone, adopted or euthanized. Conversely, he may not have even arrived at the shelter yet. It can take weeks for a concerned person to finally conclude that the cat they've been seeing around the neighborhood is actually lost and needs to be taken to a shelter. By that time, his family may have stopped looking for him.

These casual attitudes feed the euthanasia of massive numbers of so-called "lost" cats in animal shelters. The sheer volume of these animals might lead you to believe that they have no "owners," but the reality is that the millions of stray cats entering shelters came from *somewhere* – the vast majority have families, homes, people who should be missing them.

Like almost all lost cats, Roger was not wearing an ID tag. When no guardian came to claim him during his stray hold period, he was made available for adoption. He had a cold and was treated with antibiotics, but his records indicate that he had a hard time getting better in the shelter. Volunteer comments on his cage card noted "Sweet and loves attention," and "Awesome cat – likes to sit in lap and purr."

Still, after twenty-three days, no one had adopted him. When there were no more empty cages in the shelter, and still more cats were arriving at the front door, he was euthanized.

Did Roger's family miss him? Did someone mourn his loss? Does someone remember him?

"B-10"

It's hard to know what to say about this dog. He is the canine equivalent of Roger – an everyday stray dog, his story is utterly common, repeated over and over again, in shelters everywhere.

A young mixed-breed dog, he was found running loose, wearing no collar or tags, and could give no clues as to his identity. Nothing was known about him, not where he came from, who he lived with, or how he ended up lost.

No one came to look for him. He waited in kennel number B-10.

Shelter staff cared for him the best they could amongst the dozens of other animals. And alongside those other animals, he took his chances on a new home, which did not come. After two weeks in the shelter, he began to bark continuously and show the unmistakable signs of stress-induced aggression, and he was euthanized.

A perfectly nice, perfectly healthy dog. But completely anonymous. And then, gone forever.

name unknown

National statistics indicate that up to 25% of the dogs entering shelters are purebred. This comes as a surprise to many, who assume that "valuable" dogs would automatically be well cared for, never lost, and certainly not sitting amongst the homeless animals in a shelter. After all, who would pay a lot of money for a dog and then not take good care of him? Shelter workers will tell you otherwise.

This brown purebred Standard Poodle was neutered, had been recently clipped, and was wearing a green collar, but no tags. He was found on the outskirts of town, at the base of a winding road that led into the mountains, and brought to the shelter to be held for the stray hold period.

Shelters can, at their discretion, keep a dog or cat on stray hold for longer than the legally-required time period if they feel there might be a good chance the animal's guardian could show up to claim him. The staff did that for this dog, extending his hold from the minimum three days to five, and then again for one more day. Even they couldn't quite believe that no one was for looking for him.

Hidden and mostly undetected amongst the large population of strays are those who have been deliberately "lost:" unwanted animals who have been abandoned in unfamiliar neighborhoods with the naïve hope that someone will take them in, or dumped in remote areas with the callous intent that they will never be seen again. Perhaps this Poodle was one of those cases, although no one will ever know for sure. He certainly seemed stunned, almost shell-shocked, in his shelter kennel.

Finally, the staff conceded that he was not going to be claimed. The stray hold was removed and he was made available for adoption. Word of mouth reached a family in town that already included a white Standard Poodle and a black one. After everyone in the family, human and canine, met the brown Poodle, they decided to take him in. It was a happy, goofy sight: the fluffy, multi-colored pack leaving the shelter together. Whatever this Poodle's unknown past, he had been given a brand new future.

Cleopatra

Cleopatra, a beautiful cream and black Keeshond, was brought in trailing a leash from her tagless black collar. Shelter staff assumed that her guardian would quickly follow to claim her.

However, no one came during her stray hold period. Given the somewhat odd circumstances – after all, dogs do not usually enter the shelter with leashes attached to their collars as if in the middle of their daily walk – the shelter supervisor extended her stray hold in hopes that her family might still come. Cleopatra waited.

Finally, a full seven days later, just as the extended hold was to expire, her guardian called the shelter. She was ecstatic to learn that Cleopatra was there, safe. She explained that her profession kept her away from home for up to two weeks at a time and while she was gone, her father cared for Cleopatra. Somehow, Cleopatra had gotten away from him, and when his daughter called home he told her that Cleo was lost. He did not know that he should search for her at the animal shelter.

Cleopatra was extraordinarily lucky to get back home. In the many days that had passed, she could have already been adopted to another family, or worse, euthanized. Fortunately, Cleo's story has a happy ending.

What is not obvious at first glance is that Cleopatra's happy ending may involve an invisible victim. A shelter might be so full that it has to euthanize one dog to make room to take in the next. Cage space can be, and often is, that tight. Providing safety for Cleopatra could have cost another shelter animal his life.

A simple identification tag on Cleopatra's black collar could have changed the entire dynamic. The tag would have gotten her out of the shelter more quickly, or kept her from even needing to go there in the first place, freeing up valuable kennel space for another dog who needed help. When fewer animals flood animal shelters, more can be done for the ones who are already there. It may seem like a minor thing to put an ID tag on a dog or cat, but it can have an unseen ripple effect that saves lives.

name unknown

This buff-colored tabby was brought to the shelter by a woman who found him in the next county. She did not want to take him to the shelter there because it receives an extremely large number of animals and, as a result, has a very high euthanasia rate. She believed the cat would have a better chance at a shelter taking in fewer animals.

She thought she was doing the right thing, but despite her good intentions, she guaranteed one aspect of his fate: she ensured he would have virtually no chance of getting back to his home. If someone were looking for him, it would be extremely unlikely that they would include shelters in neighboring counties in their search. Transporting a lost animal even further from his home can make it difficult, even impossible, for a grieving family to find him.

Shelter staff put in a call to the cat's home county shelter, who recorded his description and location, should his family come to look for him there. But the stray hold period expired without any word, so the buff tabby was made available for adoption. He was chosen the very next day, and left the shelter to begin a totally new life – a new name, a new family, a new home in a city far away from the place he'd lived less than a week before. The phrase "nine lives" springs to mind, were it not so glib. A cat should need only one.

no name

Although this orange tabby kitten was logged in shelter records as a stray, technically she wasn't lost. She had never had a guardian to become lost from. She was a "feral" cat, never cared for within a human family, her fate virtually sealed from the start of her short, hard life.

She was only six weeks old, but already in extremely poor condition. Weak and undernourished, she had a gaping wound on her leg that had become infested with maggots. She had surely never been handled by a human, in fact, she probably had never even seen a human prior to the frightening ordeal of being caught, put in a cage, and transported to the shelter.

With a lot of dedicated, patient work, feral cats can be "tamed," but it can be a long and harrowing experience for both cat and human. Depending on how old the cat is, her background, and how long she has been on the street, the process of adapting to humans can take anywhere from a few weeks to many months. It is easiest to tame young feral kittens – if they are caught before they learn from their mothers to be afraid of humans. There is a short window of time, just a few critical weeks in a kitten's development, when she can be tamed easily. This tabby kitten had already passed that point.

She was terrified and in pain, and it was obvious that she had no one who would come to claim her during a stray hold period. As a feral cat, she would not be put up for adoption; the shelter could not give her the time and attention it would take to tame her. Given her suffering, and given that there were virtually no options for her in the shelter system, staff had the authority to override the normal stray hold, and decided to euthanize her immediately.

no name

This kitten was one of many feral cats living behind a local bakery, one of several painstakingly trapped and brought to the shelter over the course of many days by a man trying to eradicate the colony. He probably didn't realize that, given the available food source, more cats would just move in while those already there would continue to breed, replacing the cats he trapped. After all his work, in the not too distant future there would be just as many cats as when he started. In the meantime, many cats will have been trapped and put to death, and he will still have a feral cat "problem."

Managing the colony by trapping, sterilizing, vaccinating and then returning the cats would have been more effective, but this kitten and millions like her are the victims of the circumstances into which they are born. Managed colonies are a relative rarity in this country, and this kitten was not lucky enough to be part of one.

She was, instead, a "problem" to the humans around her. She was not accustomed to people, not tame, and she would not become someone's companion. She would not bring anybody the much-publicized benefits that living with companion animals brings: she wouldn't lower anyone's blood pressure or help them heal from illness, she wouldn't be teaching anyone's children about responsibility for another living being or about unconditional love, nor would she be visiting a nursing home to break through to someone who had given up on life.

But doesn't her life have value? Does she have to do something, give us something, to earn her keep, to warrant our compassion and kindness? Do we not owe her a solution that is something better than eradication? Could we not give her, and her brothers and sisters, a place in our world to live out their lives?

Molly

At many shelters, the volume of animals arriving is so large that no one animal stays very long. Those not claimed or adopted quickly are euthanized to make room for the new animals pressing through the front door. At other shelters, the community has put something of a dent in its homeless animal problem and the flood of incoming animals, although still an unrelenting flow, is not as completely overwhelming as it once was. The result is that animals may be allowed to stay at these shelters for longer periods of time – days, often weeks, and even sometimes several months – waiting for a new home.

This is good news but it comes with a downside. The longer an animal stays in a shelter, the greater the risk of a phenomenon known as "kennel stress." Despite efforts by staff and volunteers to make animals comfortable and minimize their trauma, a shelter is a highly stressful place. Already disturbed by the loss of the family and surroundings they knew, animals entering a shelter must try to adjust to a strange and frightening environment. Fear and anxiety hang in the air. They are assaulted by unfamiliar smells (to which animals are incredibly sensitive), the noise level is high, and they are continuously handled and looked at by strangers. Some are unable to eat for days. They suffer emotional trauma from continual confinement, isolation and not enough loving contact.

The symptoms of kennel stress vary. Some animals show it by becoming depressed and withdrawn while others become hyperactive. Some engage in constant barking, pacing, or panting. Others develop a fixed, glazed stare. They sometimes stop caring about their own comfort and cleanliness, smearing feces around their kennels and on themselves. They lose weight. Stressed animals are more vulnerable to illness, and once ill, have a harder time getting well. Some animals go beyond simple stress and turn a corner into what shelter workers call "kennel crazy," showing extreme behavior problems, often in the form of aggression toward other animals or humans.

The onset of kennel stress also varies – some animals develop symptoms very quickly, while others can endure for longer periods of time. Unneutered male animals, more threatened by the close proximity of other males, tend to show stress sooner than neutered males. A female in heat in a shelter can push the unneutered males to the edge more quickly. Puppies and kittens, not yet used to the comforts of a loving home, are not as affected; older, previously-pampered dogs and cats deteriorate more quickly. Individual personalities also play a part – some animals are more "laid back," some are just more sensitive.

There are ways to mitigate, to some degree, the stress shelter animals feel. Some experts in the field assert that conventional shelter design does not accommodate animals' basic needs and so is bound to traumatize them. Catering to dogs' need for companionship and space by housing them in groups in larger kennels, allowing them room to run and play and dig, and giving them access to fresh air and natural light keeps them happier and less stressed. Giving cats the quiet environment they prefer by housing them away from barking dogs, providing places to hide, ledges to sit on and different levels to climb, windows to peer out of and sunshine to lie in, will help them fend off stress. It is rare, however, to find shelters designed and operated in these ways.

Although nothing can completely eliminate the trauma and stress these sensitive beings feel, animals who receive lots of contact, who get out of their kennels to be walked or to play or to just be pet and cuddled, are better able to resist kennel stress. Many shelter staffers do as much of this as they can, but their time is limited by their other duties. Volunteers can play a key role in this area, and in fact, of all the roles that volunteers can play in a shelter, this is perhaps the most significant and most life-saving: spending time with the animals to lessen their fear, to comfort them, to increase their confidence, and to just make them feel loved.

In any case, finding a new home for an animal is always a race against time: shelter workers know they must get an animal out before kennel stress sets in. At the least, a depressed, withdrawn animal is less likely to be chosen by adopters. At worst, an animal who has become aggressive cannot be placed at all.

Molly, a stray pit bull mix, seemed miraculously unaffected by the stress of the shelter environment. She had a joyful disposition and was always happy to see a visitor at her kennel gate. Given a tennis ball, she would occupy herself contentedly in her kennel. When taken into the shelter's "play yard" by volunteers, she bounced, ran, and played tug-of-war and fetch until she wore them out.

Week after week, her sunny personality stayed the same, and she became a favorite of the staff. She had settled in as if the shelter were home and it seemed as if she would be immune to kennel stress. The staff was relieved. She was a wonderful dog, but needed more time to find the right home. Being a pit bull mix, her adopter would have to be chosen carefully. Her very long, low teats – a sign that she had been bred for many litters of puppies – were somewhat unusual looking and probably put potential adopters off. But as long as she was somehow able to escape kennel stress, she still had a chance.

When she finally did succumb, it came quickly. After months of showing virtually no interest in, much less aggression toward, other animals in the shelter, a staffer attempted to take Molly to a holiday parade to show her off and was unable to handle her. Molly could not even be walked past the other kennels without lunging at the dogs in them.

Staff looked desperately for options. Potential adopters who had earlier expressed interest in Molly were contacted again. Calls were placed to volunteer foster homes who were experienced with canine behavior problems. Perhaps if it was caught soon enough, and if she could get some time away from the shelter, Molly's deteriorating behavior could be turned around.

No adopters were interested. Experienced foster homes were full. Molly's picture had already been run in the local newspaper's "Adopt A Pet" column weeks ago to no avail. The decision was made to euthanize Molly.

The staff could not face the task. They decided to give her another week's reprieve, and scrambled to find a foster home who could work with her. While they searched, Molly deteriorated even further: her aggression intensified, and she began to direct it toward humans. There was no more hope for her here – she had gone "kennel crazy." She was undoubtedly miserable, and after nearly four months of living in the shelter, she died there.

From the staff journal in the shelter euthanasia room: "And after all this, who is made to take any responsibility? No one."

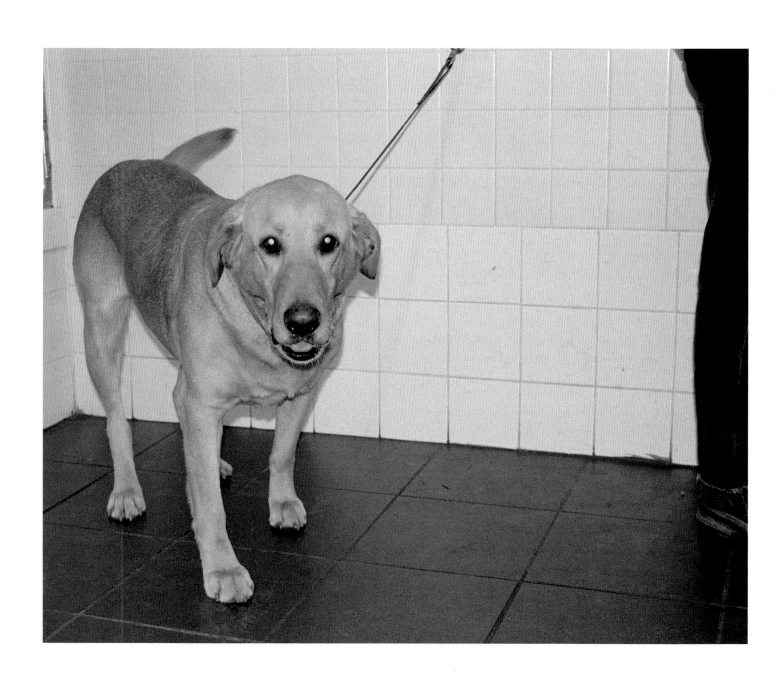

Miel

Miel's guardian was not happy that his dog was in the shelter again. It was Miel's fourth visit as a stray so the fees to reclaim him, which increase with every impoundment, were now over one hundred dollars.

As with previous episodes, Miel had been brought in by a concerned person who found him loose in the middle of a busy street. Given the number of times he had been rescued from dangerous traffic, Miel was probably lucky to be alive.

Miel's guardian, however, was very angry. In the front lobby, he argued loudly about the fees, saying they were too much, especially considering the fact the Miel would just get out again. When asked how Miel was able to keep escaping, the man offered that it was the children in the neighborhood who come to play with him after school and who opened the gate to let him out.

> *"Could you put a lock on the gate?" asked the shelter staff person.*
>
> *"No," he replied angrily, "I want the kids to be able to play with him."*
>
> *"But sir," entreated the staffer, "it's dangerous for Miel. He was picked up on a very busy street, he could be hit by a car."*
>
> *Miel's guardian shouted, "If he gets hit by a car, then that's just too bad. Then he's just another dog that gets hit by a car!"*

The lobby, filled with staff and visitors, fell silent.

Miel's guardian considered whether to pay the fees or just sign Miel over to the shelter and leave him there. Shelter staff were in a tough position: if they encouraged him to surrender his dog, Miel would have to go through the trauma of losing his family and going up for adoption to a new home. On the other hand, the staff wanted to ensure that Miel's safety would be provided for and that he would not be just another dog hit by a car. Counseling and advice were the only tools the staff had; they had to return Miel to his guardian if he wanted the dog back.

Finally, Miel's guardian decided to pay the fees. This time.

Miel, unaware that his future had been in jeopardy, that he had been just moments away from being left at the shelter, greeted his guardian with the unconditional joy that dogs show for the humans they love.

Khaky & Mackenzie

Ideally, the best function an animal shelter can serve – a true expression of the word "shelter" – is to provide safe emergency haven and temporary sanctuary for animals who have accidentally slipped past their normal safe confinement at home and become lost. If all would go as it should, a lost dog or cat would come to the shelter to receive protection just long enough for her guardian to be contacted and, with relief and gratitude that she is safe and unhurt, come and take her back home.

Khaky, a tan female pit bull, was found running down a city street and was helped to safety by an animal control officer. Wearing a collar with a current dog license, she was quickly traced to her guardian. Mackenzie was brought to the shelter by a concerned citizen who found him in a parking lot. He was wearing an ID tag imprinted with his guardian's phone numbers. Calls were placed to both families. Mackenzie was home safe and sound within hours; Khaky was home by the next morning.

It's that simple: an identification tag, a place of shelter where a lost animal can wait in safety with people who care. And it is that profound: a life no longer in jeopardy, a life saved.

Chapter 2

THE MIRACLE OF LIFE

For decades, shelters have been fighting a battle against companion animal overpopulation, the tragedy of too many puppies and kittens born into a world that cannot provide homes for them all. The statistics, however familiar to many people, are still staggering: a female dog and her puppies are theoretically capable of multiplying to over 67,000 in just six years, and a female cat and her kittens can result in over 400,000 offspring in only seven years.

The reasons for companion animal overpopulation are varied. Unintentional breeding is part of the problem – the mating of animals whose guardians didn't realize they were old enough, or didn't realize they were in heat, or just didn't take any action to prevent it. There are those who don't know about overpopulation and the need to prevent the births of more animals, and those who can't afford to spay or neuter their animal.

Intentional breeding also contributes to overpopulation, by those who let their animal have a litter because they want their children to witness the "miracle of birth," or those who are still under the outdated impression that animals *should* have one litter before being spayed.

The breeders who create and supply a market for a variety of purebred animals, and those who create non-purebred, "designer" dogs and cats, each contribute, as do those who breed their purebred as a way to recoup the purchase price of the animal or just to bring in some extra cash.

The demand in this country for purebred animals has also created a lucrative and horrific trade in living beings. It is estimated that three to five hundred thousand purebred puppies are sold in pet stores each year, and that 90% of those animals come from large-scale commercial breeders commonly referred to as "puppy mills." These mills mass-produce puppies for profit, typically keeping dozens to hundreds of female dogs in crude, cramped cages, or tied, for their entire lives. The dogs are bred incessantly, then disposed of – killed – after four or five years, when their bodies are worn out and they are no longer "productive." Their puppies are sold to brokers who ship them to other parts of the country to be resold in pet stores. The largest concentrations of puppy mills are found in the states of Arkansas, Iowa, Kansas, Missouri, Nebraska, Oklahoma, and Pennsylvania. And while the demand for purebred cats is significantly smaller than for purebred dogs, there are "kitten mills" churning out the most popular breeds: Persians, Himalayans, and Siamese.

Commercial breeders are required to be licensed, although some ignore this requirement, by the United States Department of Agriculture (USDA), and are subject to the provisions of the Animal Welfare Act, the laws which regulate the care the animals are supposed to receive. But the USDA is notoriously understaffed and inspections of puppy mills are infrequent at best. Fewer than 100 inspectors oversee over 11,000

> "My dream: to witness the birth of a tiny kitten or puppy and not have to feel sad. To be able to see a litter of newborns as the wondrous creatures that they are, not another potential victim of our society's ignorance. To know that each and every one will find and keep a loving, lifetime home. Will it ever be so?"
>
> – Shelter staff member, from the euthanasia room journal

animal facilities nationwide, which include research laboratories, circuses, zoos, and about 4,100 commercial dog breeders.

Reports of hideous conditions found in puppy mills are shockingly frequent, detailing conditions of unimaginable suffering: wire cages stacked on top of each other, feces and urine from animals on top dripping down on animals in cages below; no shelter from heat or cold; filthy, matted dogs malnourished and near starvation, with open sores and skin worn bare from rubbing against their cages, feet wounded from standing on wire for months, even years; rampant disease and illness.

The puppies born in these abysmal conditions have a high incidence of genetic defects due to careless breeding. Surveys have found that half of the puppies sold in pet stores are sick or incubating a disease. Many of the pups have behavior problems due to lack of socialization and the horrendous conditions they endure during some of the most formative weeks of their lives.

American Kennel Club (AKC) "papers" are no guarantee that a puppy did not come from a puppy mill. Contrary to what many people believe, and according to the AKC itself, it does not guarantee the health or "quality" of a dog, and does not assure that the dog came from humane conditions. The AKC is simply a registry, recording the births and lineages of dogs. The AKC does, however, take in millions of dollars each year from the registrations they process to create the papers that accompany purebred dogs, including puppy mill pups. It also opposes new legislation intended to strengthen the laws regulating puppy mills and protecting puppy mill dogs.

All of this while millions of other dogs are waiting in shelters, and dying there, for simple lack of homes. The answer is simple: when the public no longer buys into the notion that purebred dogs are the "best" dogs, when they refuse to buy puppies from pet stores, the puppy mill industry will no longer be profitable and there will be no incentive to perpetuate this brutality.

At its most basic level, as long as there are not enough homes for them all, any animal added to the existing population, for *whatever reason*, helps feed companion animal overpopulation, with devastating results. Puppies and kittens for whom homes cannot be found are brought to shelters in droves and fill the facilities beyond capacity, contributing to the euthanasia of millions. A secondary impact is borne by the adult animals in the shelter, who are in desperate need of homes but who suffer very reduced chances of getting them when they must compete with adorable puppies and kittens. Disproportionate numbers of adult animals end up as euthanasia statistics because of this disadvantage.

Spay and neuter, the solution to the companion animal overpopulation tragedy, is the impassioned battle cry of shelter workers. These routine surgical procedures sterilize dogs and cats by removing the reproductive organs of female animals (spaying) or the testicles of males (neutering). In addition to helping stop overpopulation, the animals also benefit: studies show spayed and neutered animals live longer, healthier lives with fewer medical and behavioral problems.

Animal advocates have done everything imaginable to make spay/neuter operations inexpensive, easy to obtain and desirable. Millions of flyers have been distributed extolling the many health and behavioral benefits of spaying and neutering. Countless articles have been published, and even more countless media interviews have been given. National campaigns and events have centered around the idea – a U.S. postal stamp promoting sterilization has even been released. Shelters have built low cost and free spay/neuter clinics, and some have even created mobile clinics to bring these services to the streets.

Responsible shelters also work to ensure that the animals they adopt into the community are spayed and neutered. Some collect a monetary deposit from the adopter which is refunded upon proof of sterilization, although this requires diligent and time-consuming follow-up to ensure that every adopted animal does, in fact, get spayed or neutered. Other shelters have their own clinics to perform the surgeries on site, or arrange to have the surgeries done by local veterinarians, to guarantee that adopted animals are spayed and neutered before being released to their new homes.

More recently, a new tool has been added to the arsenal fighting companion animal overpopulation: many communities across the country have adopted ordinances requiring the spaying and neutering of all dogs and cats except in very limited, designated cases.

In some areas of the country this battle has seen some success. Some shelters that once handled seemingly endless litters are finally seeing fewer, as the flood of incoming puppies and kittens has slowed. In those areas, although not completely eliminated, companion animal overpopulation is no longer the primary source of homeless animals.

The shelter in this book is one who sees many fewer litters of puppies and kittens than they did a decade ago, or even five years ago. Still, during the week these photos were taken, the number of kittens in the shelter was mind boggling, and every day of the week more arrived. This despite the fact that it was not even "kitten season" – the spring and summer months every shelter worker knows and dreads, when female cats give birth and shelters' kitten intake skyrockets to almost unimaginable levels.

And, even though there were only a handful of puppies at the shelter during the week we took photos, on a return visit eight weeks later, there were litter after litter of puppies – *dozens* of them – competing for homes that not all of them would get, a living reminder that while progress may have been made on this particular issue, there is still a long way to go.

three kittens

Five homes, ready to take in new feline family members.

Ten kittens wait in the shelter. Already, some will lose.

Outside the shelter, away from the desperate situation within its walls, a family doesn't have their cat spayed. She becomes pregnant. Gives birth to five kittens.

"We gave the other two away," the family says when they surrender the three remaining siblings at the front counter. Meaning, two of the available homes have been taken.

Only *three* homes available now. And now, *thirteen* kittens wait in the shelter.

This is how companion animal overpopulation works. Simple math, where the numbers are lives.

In reality, the numbers are tens of thousands of times larger. But the formula works just the same. *Every* new kitten added to the equation reduces the chances for others to find a home. Even the ones who don't cross the threshold of the shelter door – the ones "given away" – reduce the homes available and thus sentence other kittens to death.

Another victim in the cold mathematical formula are the scores of *adult* cats waiting in the shelter, who will be overlooked when these irresistible kitten faces peer out of the cages. According to one study, 84% of adopters want a kitten or puppy under one year old.

These three kittens were some of the lucky ones. The formula, by chance, worked out in their favor and each were adopted into new homes. They left behind many others for whom the math was not so kind.

Pumpkin Pie

Found alone and on her own, this sweet little orange tabby kitten was brought in to the shelter as a stray. She was ten or twelve weeks old and had a bad case of upper respiratory infection.

Upper respiratory infection ("URI") is not a serious illness for an otherwise healthy cat. Quite like a human cold, it is easily treatable with simple rest and recovery time, and antibiotics to prevent secondary infection. But in a shelter, time for rest and recovery is at a premium, and cats whose systems are stressed by the shelter environment can take even longer than normal to get well.

An airborne virus, URI is also quite contagious and spreads when cats sneeze. In most shelters, incoming cats are vaccinated against URI, but it takes up to two weeks to achieve full immunity, and the shots cover only some of the more common strains of virus.

Because the shelter houses large numbers of animals in a relatively small space, illness can spread quickly, making control of an outbreak difficult. Shelter staff must have a thorough knowledge of contagious illnesses like feline URI and panleukopenia, and canine distemper, parvovirus and kennel cough. They must be able to recognize symptoms, make accurate diagnoses, administer treatment, and must practice constant vigilance and dedication to careful cleaning, disinfecting and isolation procedures. If a shelter is very full, or lacks facilities to isolate sick animals, or the isolation facilities are already full, an animal with a contagious illness may be euthanized quickly to prevent an outbreak. Shelter workers know the heart-stopping feeling at the sound of a cat sneeze – the instant dread and worry that illness is breaking out, the depressing knowledge that it might mean death for the cat who sneezed, and then others if they, too, become sick.

One tool many shelters use to increase the options for animals is a foster program. Volunteers temporarily take shelter animals home, give them the care that the shelter is not able to provide, and then bring them back to the shelter to go up for adoption. Foster volunteers are a life-saving option for shelter animals. Not only can they give sick animals medical treatment and recovery time, they can give young animals time to grow up, or stressed-out animals time away from the shelter environment. Mostly, they give the one thing the animals need most and the primary thing the shelter cannot give: time.

Luckily, a family was available to foster the little orange tabby; they took her in and named her Pumpkin Pie. She had an especially miserable case of URI, was completely congested, sneezing, eyes watering and nose running constantly. The staff thought she might need two weeks of foster care, but she ended up needing another three beyond that to get fully healthy. She must have felt terrible, but she remained incredibly sweet and affectionate. By the time she was better, her foster family had become so attached to her that they decided to adopt her themselves so she could quickly get on with the business of enjoying her kittenhood.

"Neighborhood Dog"

She was a "neighborhood dog." Most people knew she was around, a few kept an eye out for her and fed her once in a while. But no one "owned" her. No one knew where she came from, only that she was there.

When she crawled up under a porch and gave birth to a litter of pups, someone decided something needed to be done and called the animal shelter.

The animal control officer who came was gentle and soothing, but the mother dog was terrified. She had to be coaxed out from under the porch. She cowered and shook.

In the truck on the ride to the shelter, she threw up something she must have eaten out of desperate hunger – it looked like a towel, or maybe a rug. Still terrified when the ride was over, she clung to the back wall of the cage, pressing her face into the corner. Again she had to be coaxed out, and once out of the truck, still shaking, she immediately scrambled underneath it, trying to hide.

The officer carried her in and got her settled in a kennel at the very back of the shelter so she could have a relatively quiet place with her pups. It would be eight weeks before the puppies would be old enough to go up for adoption, a length of time the shelter could not guarantee to any animal. Nor is the concrete kennel of a shelter the best place for puppies to grow and thrive, so the staff set about looking for a foster home who could take care of the whole family. Luckily, one was available.

The mother spent six weeks in the foster home raising her newborns into healthy, fat, bouncy puppies. During that time, she too blossomed. No longer recognizable as the terrified, cowering "neighborhood dog," she grew into a confident, happy, friendly animal. She was eager to please and seemed grateful for the comforts of a home – food, warmth, people who cared for her. When she returned to the shelter she quite expectedly suffered a brief relapse of fear and shyness, but she was able to rebound and was adopted in a week. Her puppies, too, returned to the shelter and were adopted, one by one over the course of several weeks, to new homes.

Manxie

Witness the other side of the "miracle of life."

The mother, a medium-hair black Manx, was surrendered to the shelter by her guardians because she was pregnant. In the quiet of that night, alone in her cage in the darkness, she gave birth to four manx kittens. Staff discovered them in the morning when they came to feed her.

A few days later, an orphaned one-week old kitten was brought to the shelter. Manxie, as the shelter workers had named the mother, took the orphan into her litter and cared for her along with her own babies.

Manxie took good care of her litter. But nursing and raising kittens is demanding work, and the shelter is not a good place to do it. Even though they were kept in a cage in the quiet isolation room, away from the noise and bustle of the shelter, it was stressful. Staff tried to find a foster home who could take Manxie and her kittens for the next eight weeks, an environment where they all could flourish. They also put in a call to a local Manx rescue group. While they searched, Manxie grew sick and lethargic. The kittens were not doing well either.

The mother and kittens were placed on antibiotics. But the adopted orphan, the sickest, was very thin and had stopped nursing, so the difficult decision was made to euthanize him. Three nights later, sometime in the night, Manxie watched two of her kittens die. The other two were suffering with serious upper respiratory infections.

The rescue group did not return the shelter's call and foster homes were full with other litters. The shelter was full too, and cage space was needed for more incoming animals. Manxie was not getting better, and her newborn kittens were not thriving. The staff considered all of these factors and again came to the heartbreaking decision, this time to euthanize the rest of the kittens and Manxie too.

When people say they want their children to experience "the miracle of life" by seeing the births of animals, shelter workers often become angry. Witness the other side of the "miracle," they say: see the mothers trying to take care of their offspring in the worst of conditions, striving to carry on and perpetuate life, see the tiny victims fighting to live. See the animals being born for whom there are no homes, the ones who never had a chance. This is the *other* side of the miracle of life.

"Mother Cat"

Mothers of any species are amazing beings. The mothering instinct is selfless, compassionate, ever caring, often courageous.

The man who brought in this stray gray cat said she had given birth ten days before, and that he would bring her kittens to the shelter too. After four days he was finally able to find and catch them all. Once in the shelter, hungry and weak, they came down with respiratory infections. They would need extra care and at least six more weeks with their mother before they would be old enough for adoption. The shelter was already at capacity with both adult cats and healthy, full-grown kittens. The litter quickly got sicker, and staff made the decision to euthanize the kittens, hoping the mother could still be saved.

It is never possible, of course, to know exactly what an animal is feeling, but one had to wonder... did she miss her kittens? Did she worry about them, grieve for them, alone in her cage?

Three days later, a litter of stray kittens arrived without a mother. They were only three weeks old, much too young to survive on their own, and much too young for adoption. It is an all-too-common situation, and unless someone is available to take on the time consuming job of raising them by hand, kittens like these are usually euthanized – there are just no options for them in a shelter. But staff had an idea... perhaps the mother cat, who was still lactating, would accept the orphans.

From her cage, the mother spotted the tiny kits as soon as they were brought into the room. She never took her eyes off them as the cage door was opened and, one by one, the hungry kittens were placed on the blanket in front of her. She cleaned them as they cried, then laid down for them to nurse from her swollen teats. Despite what grief or confusion she herself might have been going through, she remained a mother first and foremost, accepting the litter of orphans, and in doing so, gave them their very survival. If these generous acts had been performed by a human being, we would call her heroic.

Now, all she and the kittens needed was time.

There are rarely enough foster homes for all the animals who need them. Availability changes on a day-by-day basis – once a foster family brings an animal back to the shelter, they then have room to take in another. No home had been available for the mother and her own kittens a week before, but during the week, space had opened up. The mother and her adopted litter moved in, and six weeks later the kittens returned, healthy and grown-up. Each was adopted within a few days. The mother cat was spayed, then she too returned, ready for, and so very deserving of, a new, permanent home.

She was adopted two weeks later, to begin a life where heroics are not required – where just being a cat is plenty enough.

Buddy

Being a purebred dog doesn't mean that life will be easy.

Buddy was a chocolate Labrador Retriever given up by his guardian. He was happy by nature, and staff who assessed his temperament noted, "He's an active, high energy dog with quite a bit of training, he sits on command and walks well on a leash. He's an exuberant dog who loves to play, likes attention and shows no aggression."

Given his very popular breed, staff assumed he would be adopted quickly. They put his photo on the shelter website, and talked to potential adopters. Some were interested, but Buddy's high energy level gave them pause.

As the days wore on, Buddy waited for the right adopter. Surely someone would want a dog like him; surely a chocolate Lab wouldn't go unadopted. But the longer Buddy waited, the more his energy and exuberance turned on him. He was unhappy without consistent contact and attention. He did not like being confined and alone. He needed companionship. He began barking continuously and nothing shelter staff did to discourage him would get him to stop.

Staff worked to find a way to get him out before his behavior deteriorated further. They tried to find a foster home who could take him for a respite, and also put in a call to the regional Labrador Retriever breed rescue group. The group wanted to help, but they had no room for Buddy. Along with the unwanted Labs they were already caring for, they were overwhelmed with fifty-seven new dogs who had recently been seized by authorities from a breeder keeping them in inhumane conditions.

Finally, Buddy got lucky. An adopter came to meet him, referred to the shelter by the rescue group. The adopter was prepared to see him through the behavior problems Buddy had developed while in the shelter, and wanted to bring him back to the exuberant, happy dog he once was.

One would think that a chocolate Lab would have no problem finding a home. Or keeping it. Or even getting a new one, if he had to. Surprising as it may seem, there are just no better guarantees for a dog like Buddy than for any other homeless animal.

"The Picnic Gang"

Root Beer is a brave little kitten who always wants to know what's happening. Kitten-proofing your house is a good idea with this curious boy.

Cream Soda loves to play and run around with his brother. He really enjoys the company of other cats, and would do well in a multi-cat household.

Ginger Ale is the most independent of the three brothers... he can be a little shy, so an active house with small children might not be the best place for him.

Potato Salad is a mellow lap-cat who would rather sit and watch others play than get involved. If you are looking for a calm kitten who is mature beyond his years (or weeks!), this is your cat. He came to the shelter a tiny, wild, flea- and parasite-infested kitten with a cold and therefore is smaller than others of his age.

Cole Slaw loves to wrestle with his fellow felines... he might not be great for a house with small children, as he is a rough-and-tough kitty. However, under the tough exterior lies a heart of pure gold....

It would be easy to view all kittens as somewhat the same: endlessly playful, high-spirited, wide-eyed balls of fluff whose goal in life is to have as much fun as possible. And indeed, life in the world of kittens probably is a lot like that. But these seemingly similar little creatures are definitely individuals with their own distinct temperaments, preferences and behaviors. Even as very young kittens, their unique personalities are already developing.

These kittens arrived at the shelter in two separate litters of strays, but at only six weeks old, were too young to go up for adoption. Often, kittens this young, especially strays, are "unsocialized" – not yet accustomed to being part of a human household, not yet old enough to have fully learned cat behavior from their littermates. Being removed from their mother so early can also compromise their health and immune system, so they do much better if they can get a little older and stronger before moving into the stressful shelter environment.

A shelter staff person took the kittens home to give them the extra time and socialization they needed. When she brought them back three weeks later, she knew each of them individually and posted the detailed "introduction" on their cage door. It was a tremendous advantage to both the kittens and their potential adopters, who could see the kind of personality they might be bringing home with them.

In the shelter system, where high volumes of animals are handled in a short time, knowing each animal in depth is a luxury that is seldom possible. Nonetheless, it is a luxury that every animal deserves: to be known, and respected, as the unique individual he is.

Sadly, Potato Salad was diagnosed with liver failure shortly after re-entering the shelter, and was euthanized. The rest of the Picnic Gang were happily adopted to new homes.

puppy & kitten

A single unspayed dog or cat gives birth to a litter of babies. Each of her babies who are not spayed or neutered create more babies, and the members of those litters go on to create more. Because animals give birth in litters, overpopulation grows exponentially as it progresses through the generations. Shelters today are filled with the offspring of the offspring of the offspring who bear its tragic legacy. Yet, it is easily stopped. One animal at a time, the progression can be halted in its tracks, the legacy ended.

This Rottweiler mix puppy, only five weeks old and barely weaned, was found alone in a park. He arrived at the shelter via two teenagers who patched together several dilapidated cardboard boxes to carry him in. After a three week stay in foster care, he was old enough to go up for adoption.

The kitten on the next page, just a few months old, was found on her own by kind people who brought her to the shelter. Her bi-color eyes, one blue and one green, were startling and gave her an exotic look.

Luckily, both of these adorable creatures found homes quickly. As a condition of their adoptions (as with all adoptions from the shelter) the puppy would be neutered and the kitten spayed.

The puppy will be a healthier dog, with a longer, safer life, for having been neutered. He will be less likely to become lost because he will have less desire to wander from home: of the dogs hit by cars, 80% are unneutered males – they can smell a female in heat several miles away, and their urge to get to that female is so strong that they are oblivious to the dangers of streets and cars. His chance of prostate problems, including cancer, as well as his chances of urinary problems that lead to kidney disease, will be vastly reduced, and he will not suffer testicular cancer.

In most communities, his dog license will be less expensive, a reflection of the reality that unneutered and unspayed dogs create more animal control work and expense to the public than dogs who are sterilized.

He'll be less territorial toward other male dogs, so he'll be less likely to get into fights. He'll not likely develop the habits of marking his territory with urine and mounting legs and other objects. Without the distraction of protecting territory, he'll be happier, more content, and more focused on his human family and a better companion to them. Similarly, male cats who are neutered at an early age do not develop the habit of "spraying": marking their territory – which, in a home, is walls, furniture, and carpets – with urine. They'll have fewer fights with other male cats, and will thus avoid the bite injuries that are a primary way cats catch various contagious and deadly diseases.

The white kitten will live a happier and healthier life for having been spayed. Her risk of breast cancer will be drastically reduced. She will not go into heat (up to three times a year, up to fifteen days each time), yowling and attracting neighborhood male cats as she tries frantically to escape from the house. She'll be calmer and more comfortable, and a better companion to her family. Likewise, a female dog who is spayed before her first heat is 200 times less likely to develop breast cancer and will also avoid the uterine infection pyometra, common in older unspayed dogs. Because she will not go into heat, her family will be spared the messy twice-yearly estrus cycle when she passes blood and other fluids.

Some people worry that it is "unnatural" to spay or neuter companion animals. But our companion animals have to live in our world, a less than natural environment for them, where sexual maturity and close proximity to large numbers of other animals creates a continual battle of physical drives, and a constant assault on their senses and instincts. It is stressful, and unaltered animals reveal it with a higher incidence of behavior and temperament problems. Unneutered male dogs, for instance, are *three times* more likely to bite than neutered dogs. If we are going to ask animals to live with us as companions in *our* world, do we not owe it to them to do everything we can to make them comfortable and provide for their safety?

The kitten and puppy from this shelter will be spayed and neutered before reaching sexual maturity. A major advancement in veterinary medicine, "early age spay/neuter" involves sterilizing animals when they are as young as eight weeks of age, instead of waiting until the previous traditional age of six months or even older. Although this may at first sound somewhat radical, studies show no adverse side affects from early age spay/neuter. In fact, they show that younger animals have less difficulty recovering from anesthesia and fewer post-operative complications.

Waiting to spay/neuter at a later age courts disaster by creating a critical juncture of timing. Animals, especially cats, can mature and reproduce as early as five months of age. Many breed before their guardians are able to, or even think to, arrange for their sterilization. Wide use of early age spay/neuter would be a tremendous boon in reducing these accidental breedings and the homeless litters they create.

By being spayed and neutered, these two young animals will not perpetuate the situation into which they were born. Their spay and neuter will prevent the births of potentially thousands of dogs and cats into an already overpopulated world. The legacy of companion animal overpopulation, and its tragic consequences, will not be handed down. Right here, right now, one small kitten and one tiny puppy bring us one powerful step – actually, two steps – closer to ending the legacy of companion animal overpopulation.

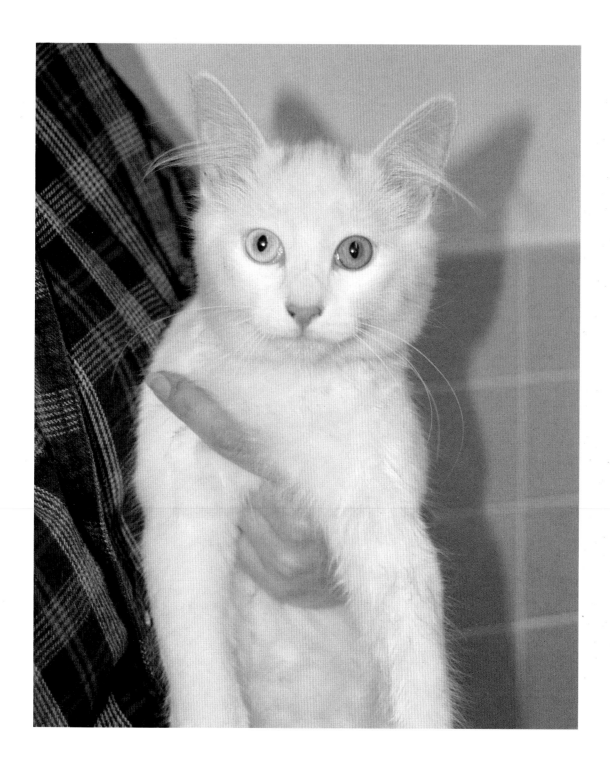

Chapter 3

REASON FOR SURRENDER

On every shelter intake form, there is a fateful blank space waiting to be completed. Labeled "reason for surrender," it will describe, in just a few short words, a pivotal turn in an animal's life: why his guardian has made the decision to voluntarily relinquish him to the shelter. A myriad of reasons will be recorded in this space, some serious, others trivial. The most common reasons are pre-programmed into shelter computer systems, a litany of ways in which animals fail to measure up to our expectations and ways in which our own life changes do not accommodate them.

It is one of the major functions of shelters to accept animals who, for whatever reason, are no longer wanted by their guardians. About one-third of the animals entering shelters nationwide are there because they have been surrendered.

Surrendering an animal is a remarkably simple process: the guardian brings in the animal and signs a form which transfers permanent, legal ownership of the animal to the shelter. Some, but not all, shelters require a fee or ask for a donation, not only to help cover some of the expenses that will be incurred to care for the animal, but also to reinforce a message of accountability – that there should be some cost for abandoning a responsibility.

Many shelters also ask the guardian to fill out a "personality profile," a form documenting the animal's disposition and habits, likes and dislikes, compatibility with other animals, experience with children, medical history, and any other information that will help the shelter match the animal to a new, and hopefully *this* time permanent, home.

Some surrenders are made without the benefit of this helpful information. It is a fairly common occurrence for shelter workers, upon arriving at work in the morning, to find animals who have been left in the middle of the night on the doorstep or tied to a tree or just dropped off and left loose on the grounds. Resigned to this inevitability, some shelters provide nighttime "drop boxes" so that people who are too embarrassed or ashamed to surrender their animals directly to staff can leave them safely, and, anonymously. Other shelters feel that this goes too far, making it simply too easy to "dump" an animal and invoking the unsettling and insulting image of Goodwill collection boxes for "used goods."

However he is surrendered, and for whatever reason, it is now a matter of life and death for the animal. He has lost his home, his security, his safety. He has lost everything, and now may ultimately lose his life.

> Sheds... destructive... barks... can't contain... digs... can't control....
>
> Divorce... new baby... going on vacation... moving....
>
> Boyfriend doesn't like... new job... gift... allergies....
>
> Not enough time for... too expensive... too much work....
>
> Too old... too many... too big... too small....
>
> Don't want anymore....

The voluntary surrender of companion animals is, to many people, the most incomprehensible part of the homeless animal problem. Many guardians just can't *conceive* of willingly giving up their animal friends, for *any* reason, especially knowing that it could lead to the animal's death. Some of the reasons given for surrendering animals seem almost unbelievable, but spend a day behind the receiving counter of an animal shelter and you will almost certainly develop a disheartening awareness of the lesser side of human nature.

Which also makes it perhaps the most discouraging aspect of the homeless animal problem. Surrenders blatantly demonstrate some of the basic attitudes that create the need for animal shelters in the first place: a lack of commitment by some people toward the animals they have taken into their lives; a disconnection from an animal as a living, feeling being; an unwillingness to be inconvenienced by an animal's needs; surprisingly unrealistic expectations about how an animal will fit into day to day life; the quintessential attitude of disposability. And, it is probably the most difficult part of the homeless animal problem to solve: how does one address such fundamental attitudes?

There are some surrenders which are caused by nearly insurmountable problems. Rental housing allowing animals is, in many cities, an increasingly rare commodity, and many, many animals are surrendered because their guardians cannot find a landlord who will allow their companions. Animals sometimes become ill and need veterinary treatment that their guardians cannot afford. And in the saddest cases, animals are surrendered when their guardians experience life tragedies, or become ill, or have died, and there is no one to care for their companions.

Still, the vast majority of surrenders are not the result of unavoidable circumstances. Studies show that most surrendered animals haven't even been in the home a full year. Half of surrendered animals are not spayed or neutered, and many have never been to a veterinarian. About a third have lived outdoors all or almost all of the time and the vast majority of surrendered dogs have received no training whatsoever. Animals acquired from friends are surrendered in larger numbers than animals acquired from other

sources. The most commonly cited reasons for surrender have to do with preventable animal behavior problems, or life changes for the guardian. These findings suggest a basic underlying dynamic: that the decision to acquire an animal was made casually, without much forethought and planning, or that it was an uninformed decision.

All of which points to a critical need for education and information. Many shelters are realizing that their role must change, and change rather profoundly: as much as finding *new* homes for homeless animals, shelters need to find ways to help animals keep the homes they already have. They must help potential new guardians understand the commitment they are making before they bring an animal into their lives. Many shelters are working at becoming resources to their communities, providing the much-needed education, information and assistance that will help *prevent* surrenders.

A handful of shelters have developed innovative "pet parenting" classes that help people learn, *before* they get an animal, how to select one who will be compatible with them and their lifestyle. They teach about the care and time animals need. They help prospective guardians think ahead to the changes that will take place in their lives and how they will accommodate an animal during those changes.

Others shelters are building programs designed to educate *after* the animal goes home. These programs intervene and help solve problems before they escalate to surrender. Many people simply do not have the knowledge or expertise to deal constructively with animal behavior problems, and to know that most behavior problems are actually quite preventable or solvable. Some shelters provide low-cost or free training classes to teach both guardian and animal how to work together to avoid problems. Others have animal behaviorists on staff who will consult with a family to help them understand their animal's behavior, the causes of behavior problems and how to work through and solve those problems. A recent study found that dogs are 90% less likely to be surrendered when their guardians have access to behavioral advice.

To help with housing problems, some shelters provide guidance on rentals and landlords. To help with financial issues, some distribute information about health insurance available for animals. Others offer loans for unexpected veterinary costs so that an animal's illness doesn't create financial problems so severe they result in the animal's surrender.

These kinds of innovative outreach programs are fairly new – not many shelters have such programs, and those that do have implemented them only in recent years. The programs represent a significant shift in perspective for shelters. After all, the shelter system is by definition set up to deal with animals *after* they have become homeless: to take them in, care for them, try to save them and find them a new home. For shelters to realize that much of the answer to the homeless animal problem lies in preemptive action, that it is possible, even *necessary*, to save animals they will never actually see or lay hands on, is a fairly radical change in thinking. And even for those shelters who understand this, time and money are limiting factors. It can be difficult for shelters deluged with already-homeless animals to allocate resources to programs of prevention.

At a deeper level, the surrender problem is rooted in the way society views and places value on companion animals. Animals, despite the fact that they are living, feeling beings, are defined legally and through the general consensus of society as property – as *possessions*. Anyone can get an animal, and everyone has the "right" to have whatever animal they choose. Although people are screened and counseled when adopting from a shelter, animals of all kinds are easily obtainable from many other sources – such as pet stores, breeders, friends, and "free to a good home" ads in the newspaper – without having to prove to anyone a level of commitment to the animal or an educated understanding of what that commitment means. Just ante up the money, if there even is a price, and like any other piece of property, the object of desire can be had.

And, just as easily, that property can be disposed of, with no consequences – a municipal shelter will have to take the animal when a reason for surrender is stated and ownership is signed over. Our society simply does not require anything more, any deeper consideration, when it comes to companion animals.

There is a moment, when the paperwork has been completed, and the animal is being handed over to shelter staff... if you watch carefully, you can sometimes see the exact moment when the animal comprehends what is happening, when he finally realizes that his guardian is leaving and he is staying; the exact moment when the confusion in his eyes is replaced by understanding, and then turns to panic, desperation. Sadness, that will turn to grief as the days unwind, while he waits for another chance that may or may not come.

Jake

REASON FOR SURRENDER: "Unable to care for."

Although most surrenders are preventable, tragedy is a fact of life. Unexpected things happen, people become ill, lives fall apart. And when those people have an animal, the animal's life also falls apart.

Some humane organizations offer planning kits and advice on how to provide for your animal companions after your death or in the event you become incapacitated. But it is hard enough to make the plans we all know we should – wills, trusts, powers of attorney, instructions, financial arrangements. It does not occur to most of us that we need to make arrangements for our animals too.

Jake was found stray, but was wearing a dog license. The license was traced to an address, and when an animal control officer went there, a friend of Jake's guardian answered the door. The friend told the officer that Jake's guardian had had a breakdown a few days ago and could not be contacted. Distressed, but apparently unable to care for Jake herself, she signed Jake over to the shelter on his guardian's behalf.

Given the magnitude of the homeless animal problem, shelters do not have the room to house animals whose guardians are having a crisis and need time to get back on their feet. Sadly, when people have no support network, when they are "falling through the cracks," their animals fall with them. In a handful of communities, programs exist to take in the animals of battered women, so that the women can leave their abusive situations knowing their animals are safe (many abusers also harm, or threaten to harm, the family dog or cat as a way to intimidate the women and keep them from leaving), but such programs are rare and generally do not have the resources to extend to other kinds of life crises.

Shelter staff would have preferred to speak directly with Jake's guardian to confirm that the information was accurate, that he could not care for Jake, and that no other friends or family might be able to take Jake in. They held Jake for seven days after the surrender to give his guardian time to come forward; they also tried to locate him through a number of local agencies, but were unsuccessful, and so decided to accept the friend's surrender as official and make Jake available for adoption.

In his kennel, Jake was scared and nervous. A staff person assessing his temperament had to work patiently with him to get past what seemed like defensive, perhaps aggressive, behavior to find the sweet, shy dog underneath. Jake was a bit wary of men, did not seem to enjoy being petted and had no concept of a leash, but he readily responded to kindness and gentle direction, quickly learning "sit" and "down." "Needs a home to build his confidence with treats and love," the staff person noted in his records.

Happily for Jake, that home appeared. Tragedy turned, and Jake would have the chance to feel loved and safe, allowed to grow into the happy dog he was meant to be.

Sadie

REASON FOR SURRENDER: "Moving."

This is one of the most commonly cited reasons for surrender of dogs and cats. For many people it is simply not a high priority to bring along their companions when they move. There are others who, given their transitory lifestyle or situation, probably should never have gotten an animal. Shelters in communities with a college or military base often deal with very high numbers of animals left behind.

But for many people, especially in cities where the vacancy rate is low, and especially for lower income animal guardians, finding rental housing that allows companion animals can be difficult at best, and the search agonizing. There are effective strategies animal guardians can use to increase their attractiveness to potential landlords: offering an additional security deposit; creating an animal "resume" highlighting the animal's good behavior and the guardian's responsible animal care; providing references from past landlords. Some shelters help with programs that reach out to property owners, encouraging them to consider animal guardians as renters, or maintain listings of animal-friendly landlords for renters. But even with such tactics, housing issues can be very challenging and often result in heartbreak – when guardians resort to new homes that do not allow their companions, the animals are left homeless.

Sadie's guardians moved to a place that did not allow cats. Now five years old, she had lived her whole life with them as a protected, completely indoor cat. She ate in the kitchen and slept on the bed. Now she had to make the difficult transition from this safe, comfortable life, to the uncertain life of a shelter animal. Somehow, she was able to do so.

Staff worked to find her a new home. They put her photo in the paper and showed her off at the local outlet of a national pet supply chain that, instead of selling animals, works with community shelters to facilitate adoptions of homeless animals.

The staff's efforts paid off. Three weeks later, Sadie was adopted. She too, would now be "moving," but on to a new life and a second chance for a lifelong, stable home.

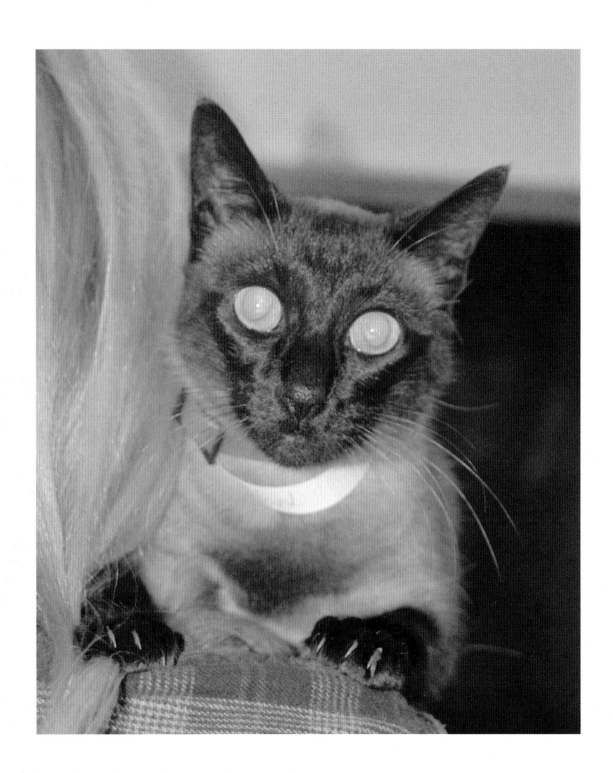

Willow

REASON FOR SURRENDER: "Can't keep, allergies."

Allergies are the second most cited reason for surrender of cats. Contrary to popular opinion, human allergies to animals are not caused by the animals' fur, but by dander – proteins in the saliva and skin which are shed from the animal. Some breeds are said to cause less reaction, but most experts agree that there are no particular breeds which are more or less allergenic.

Many people with allergies can, with some work and dedication, live with animal companions. The animal's dander can often be reduced to tolerable levels with food additives, frequent brushing, bathing and sprays or "wipes" which are applied to the animal's fur. Frequent vacuuming and washing of bedding and household surfaces helps. Allergy medications also provide relief for many people.

Still, Willow was surrendered by her family.

Shelter staff immediately put in a call to a "breed rescue" group: an organization of volunteers who share an affection for a particular breed of animal, in this case, Siamese cats. These groups take purebred animals from shelters, place them with their own foster volunteers who provide temporary care, then adopt the animals to new homes. Good breed rescue groups have expertise about their favored breed and are diligent in ensuring new homes are compatible with the breed's unique needs and characteristics. For virtually every dog and cat breed there is a rescue group. And for those who want a specific breed of animal for a companion, rescue groups offer the chance to give a desperately needed home to a homeless animal, rather than supporting more breeding by buying from a pet store or breeder.

Without question, breed rescue means more animals saved and more open shelter space that can help other animals in need. But the relationship between breed rescue groups and shelters can be tense. Shelters, who struggle to promote the idea that every animal is valuable, see breed rescue as demonstrating the notion that certain animals are more worthy of saving than others, based solely on the arbitrary criteria of their breed. Nonetheless, many shelters set aside philosophical differences and work closely with breed rescue groups to give homeless animals one more option for a happy ending.

Although undeniably beautiful, Willow was an aloof cat. As she entered her third week at the shelter, she became depressed and lethargic, which only added to her appearance of disinterest. If her fate had been based on her behavior and personality alone, she most likely would have been passed over by potential adopters. But Willow had been born into a shape and colors we call Siamese, and that saved her – the local Siamese breed rescue group would find her a home.

Of course she deserved no less. She deserved to be saved. And, of course, so did every cat in the shelter.

Misha

REASON FOR SURRENDER: "Abandoned by owner."

Misha's guardian was moving to Oregon. She left Misha in the temporary care of a co-worker, promising to return for her in a week. One and a half months later, she still had not returned. Unable to keep Misha any longer, the co-worker brought her to the shelter.

Shelter staff attempted to track Misha's guardian in Oregon, but could not get a forwarding address or new phone number. With no leads, Misha was now alone.

It is difficult enough to imagine what life's changes will bring five, or ten years down the line; it is even more difficult to imagine how to accommodate an animal when those changes come along. But an animal's fate rests on that very consideration.

Throughout their lives, many companion animals bounce from guardian to guardian, from home to home to home. A stunning statistic: only one animal in three has a home that lasts their entire lifetime. For the others, millions of them, they are left behind, or given away, or surrendered to shelters, while their guardians move on, assuming, wanting to believe, convincing themselves, that somehow their animals are fine. The reality is, many are not.

Misha spent three weeks in the shelter, then began to show signs of kennel stress. "She was probably a feisty pup to begin with and being kenneled has not helped," a shelter staff person noted in her records. "She is very mouthy and nippy and does not seem to do well with other dogs. This dog would need an experienced guardian without small children."

A week later, Misha's stress had gotten much worse. "She is going kennel crazy here," the animal care supervisor noted in Misha's records. "Disposition for euthanasia."

"Sorry, we tried."

Sox

REASON FOR SURRENDER: "We are getting too old to take care of him."

When Sox's guardians surrendered him to the shelter, they filled out the form describing his personality and habits to give potential adopters more information about him. According to their entries, Sox was friendly and playful, liked children and other animals, and had no behavior problems. He had come to them as a stray, but he must have lived with someone else before them because he was already neutered.

There is sometimes a fine line in people's minds when making a commitment to an animal. Most legal definitions say that an animal belongs to you if you care for him for thirty days. If an animal arrives as a stray, often that label seems to stick forever. Even years later, people feel that because they didn't *intentionally* acquire him, because he just "showed up," that they don't really have *responsibility* for him. How long does a "stray" animal have to remain a stray?

Sox was with this family two years, and although he lived with them in their house, played with their grandchildren and seemed to cause them no trouble, perhaps they still considered him a stray, and didn't consider him "theirs." They'd never taken him to see a veterinarian, and at some point, decided that they could no longer care for him.

It took two weeks, but Sox was again adopted, into at least his *third* home, and hopefully his *last*.

Cisco

REASON FOR SURRENDER: "Will not contain."

Aneighbor called animal control to report Cisco running loose on their street and behaving threateningly towards passers-by.

Cisco's guardian came to the shelter to reclaim him, but his conversation with staff was brief and belligerent. He simply didn't see a problem and was unwilling to contain Cisco, either for his own safety or the safety of others. Instead, he signed the dog over to the shelter and left.

Cisco, tied on a leash in the receiving area, growled at anyone who approached him.

Not every animal who is surrendered to a shelter gets a chance at adoption. Once the animal is signed over, the shelter has sole discretion in deciding what the next step will be. If the shelter is extremely full, or the animal has health or temperament problems, or if it's just simply unlikely that he will be adopted, he can be euthanized without ever going up for adoption. There are just no guarantees, something shelter workers try desperately to make the public understand – if you surrender your animal, his life will be at risk.

Animal behaviorists tell us aggression in dogs is largely a function of upbringing. Dogs are like children, in that what they do, or do not, receive in their formative months can create lifelong behavioral patterns. Cisco's aggression likely could have been prevented with the socialization and training that all puppies need.

A second chance for Cisco was not a possibility. What potential adopter would be able and willing to provide for a dog who may be aggressive? Although in theory it might have been possible, in practical application, even if such an adopter appeared, a shelter cannot adopt out a dog with a history of aggression. Cisco's guardian still had the option of taking him home and confining him to keep him from being a danger, but chose not to, and so, having been surrendered, Cisco now had no options.

Cisco was taken straight from the receiving area to the euthanasia room.

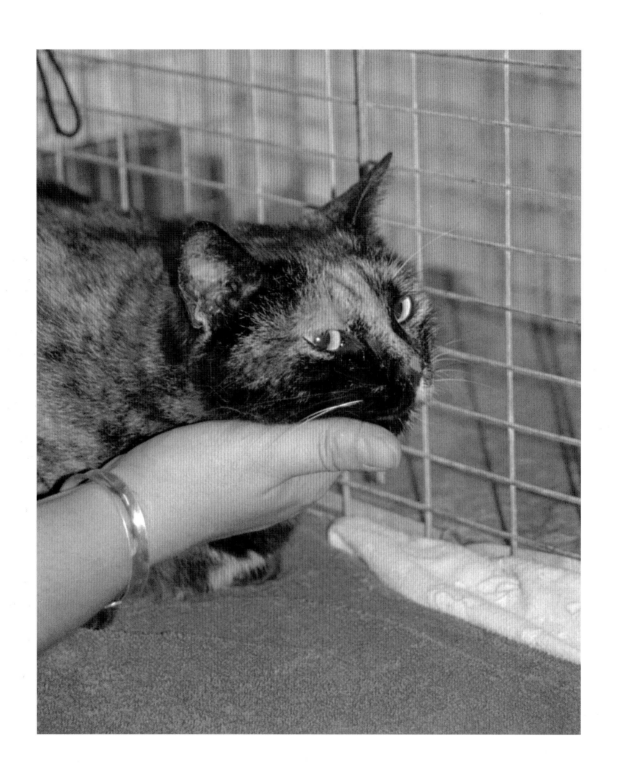

Skylar

REASON FOR SURRENDER: "Skittish, displaced our other cat, moved to a smaller home."

Skylar, a beautiful adult tortoise shell cat, was surrendered by her guardians, even though they had another cat whom they were keeping. On her personality profile, they indicated she had lived with them for nearly four years. She was "skittish by day, very affectionate by night." Skylar was scared of confined places, they said, and didn't like being picked up or held, but *"loves* to be petted in the evening, after she's climbed up next to us on the bed or couch. She gets on ok with our other cat, though sometimes dominates and defends her backyard territory from neighborhood cats." She didn't scratch the furniture, she came when her name was called, and she slept with them at night.

Reading these various entries on her profile, one begins to get a sense of Skylar's life: nervous and on guard during the bustle of daytime, she seems to relax in the quiet of the evening, feeling safe, seeking affection and finding comfort with her human family. What one does *not* get from reading the profile, however, is a clearly compelling reason for giving her up... is "skittish" the reason for removing her from their lives? Or occasionally fighting with their other cat, as many cats do?

With a personality like Skylar's, entering the stressful shelter environment was nothing less than traumatic. Shelters who can afford the time will allow a newly-received animal a "cooling down" period to get over her initial fear and begin to adapt to shelter life. Some animals simply cannot do it.

The final comments from Skylar's family on her personality profile say, ironically, "she needs patience and TLC," things they themselves were apparently no longer willing to give her. They concluded, "she really needs to be the sole cat in a home." They may have sincerely wanted these things for Skylar, but unfortunately, a skittish, traumatized cat in a shelter is highly unlikely to be selected by potential adopters.

Even after three days of "cooling down," Skylar continued to be so terrified that shelter staff decided to euthanize her, rather than let her wait, scared and suffering, for the extremely remote possibility of a second chance.

Sadi

REASON FOR SURRENDER: "Adopted two weeks ago. Runs away."

From Sadi's shelter records: "Sadi is being returned because she cannot be confined. New guardian was not willing to try keeping her in – he lets her out in the morning and she hops the fence. He is used to having dogs in a certain set-up and Sadi did not come 'ready made.' I tried to express the importance of working through the adjustment period, but he does not feel she will ever change or learn."

Many people are surprised by the adjustment period an adopted animal can need. Caught up in the joy of welcoming a new member to the family, expectations run high and it is easy to forget that, for the animal, a new home can be a difficult life change. Being in the shelter is already an experience that leaves many animals shaken and confused. They may also be grieving for the people who, to them, are inexplicably gone from their lives – animals remember, even years later, people they've known.

At their deepest nature, dogs are "pack" animals and their emotional well-being is rooted in living in a group with others they know and count on. For domestic dogs, the "pack" is the family they live with, and every change of home translates to a confusing and stressful change in their most basic social structure and emotional foundation. A sensitive dog can be quite affected, losing confidence and her sense of security. It gets harder and does more damage to her psyche each time she has to go through it again.

In a new home, a dog does not automatically know what is expected of her. It takes time to learn her place in the "pack," to form bonds, to become accustomed to new rules and routines, and to regain a feeling of safety and stability. It can be a tenuous time during which she will need gentleness, patience, and realistic expectations from her new guardians. Many adoptions fail during this critical period, as did Sadi's.

Five days after Sadi returned, a staffer noted, "Sadi is very depressed, not looking good emotionally." Fortunately, a young couple who had adopted a dog from the shelter some years ago decided to adopt another. They met Sadi and began to love her right away. The shelter staffer knew that if Sadi were returned to the shelter again, she would probably not hold up to the strain. "Be careful, she's under stress," he counseled, almost pleading with them to understand, "she's been here, then left, then came back... she needs someone who will *be* with her." The couple listened carefully and understood, committed to helping Sadi through yet another major adjustment in her life, and to making it the last one she would have to go through.

They brought their other dog, a ten year old black retriever mix, to meet Sadi. In the shelter courtyard, the new pack – white dog, black dog, two humans – was formed, their bond already growing. They left the shelter together, the older dog walking closely at Sadi's side, seeming to sense that she needed friendship and comfort. In the car, Sadi looked uncertain, but she didn't know, yet, that she finally had a stable and happy future ahead of her.

Chapter 4

In the Arms of a Stranger

Although everyone, shelter workers included, would like to focus on happy endings and successes, any picture of the homeless animal problem and the animal sheltering system would not be complete or accurate without also acknowledging, and understanding, euthanasia.

In the past, animal shelters have downplayed the euthanasia they perform, knowing that most people do not want to hear about it, and even become angry or offended when told about it. Shelters often are blamed for the message when in fact they are just the messenger. But in recent years, many shelters have come to realize that their communities cannot change what they can't see, and so have embraced strategies of openness and honesty about euthanasia, being clear, truthful and often graphic. And indeed, some members of their communities are angered and offended by the information. As they *should* be – using euthanasia as a solution to the homeless animal problem is abhorrent.

The truth is, euthanasia does happen, to *millions* of animals each year, and it does no one, least of all the animals, any good to pretend it doesn't, or to downplay or minimize it. Turning away from this reality is a betrayal of the animals. If they must go through it, surely we can be strong enough to know about it and face it.

At the shelter in this book, this is how it happens, a sad mix of clinical procedure and tender mercy.

As in most shelters, there is a room set aside specifically for euthanizing animals. Some of the shelter's staff members are specially trained and certified to perform euthanasia. Within that group, the job is assigned on a rotating basis, an attempt to reduce the stress by giving staff a break from the task. Most days, there are animals to be euthanized. Some days it's one or two, other days it can be as many as twenty or more.

The drug used, and the accepted standard within the shelter field for physically humane euthanasia, is sodium pentobarbital. Sodium pentobarbital is a powerful sedative which is given in an overdose quantity to cause quick and painless loss of consciousness, followed by depression of the brain centers that control breathing and blood pressure, and finally, stopping of the heart. Although sodium pentobarbital has therapeutic uses for animals and humans, it is formulated specifically for animal euthanasia by several drug companies under the unsettling names of Fatal-Plus, Euthasol, Sleepaway, and Socumb.

> "Our policy: to tell the truth. Our goal: to change the truth we have to tell."
>
> — California animal shelter

The federal Drug Enforcement Administration classifies sodium pentobarbital as a "Schedule II controlled substance," so shelters must be licensed to obtain and use it, and must follow strict storage and record-keeping procedures. Every milliliter used is logged in detail and signed for by the staff person who used it.

Beyond ensuring a physically humane death, staff do all they can to make euthanasia psychologically humane as well. They work slowly and quietly to create a calm atmosphere in the euthanasia room, and strive to keep their own emotions under control so that an animal doesn't feel their sadness and anger. An animal is never euthanized within sight of another animal, and each dead animal is removed before the next live animal is brought into the room. If an animal is aggressive or very nervous, a pre-euthanasia tranquilizer is given to relax him. Staff speak softly to the animals throughout the process, holding them and petting them, until each animal is gone.

Most of the animals euthanized are dogs and cats, but it is a sad reality that every species of animals which humans keep as "pets" will at some point be euthanized in the shelter. There are differing procedures and methods for euthanizing rabbits, guinea pigs, mice, birds, ferrets, lizards, snakes, and pot bellied pigs. Shelter workers must carry with them the terrible knowledge of how to bring death to a wide variety of creatures.

Staff work in pairs when euthanizing animals. One worker prepares the injection, while the other worker brings the animal into the room. Together they perform an extensive ritual of final double-checks to make certain that no mistakes have been made. They match the control number on the euthanasia list to the number on the animal's collar. They compare the description of the animal on the paperwork to the animal himself. They scan a lost animal one last time to ensure a microchip has not been missed and examine him once more to make sure an identifying tattoo has not gone unnoticed. They re-check computer records to make sure no one has missed a clue as to a lost animal's guardian or missed a person who might have expressed interest in adopting him. They make absolutely sure that this is the right animal, and that every possible option they can offer him has been exhausted.

For dogs, one worker positions herself behind the dog and wraps an arm gently but firmly around him, using her free hand to hold his leg and apply pressure to the vein. The other worker quickly shaves a small patch of fur, locates the vein, then slides the needle in and pushes the plunger to send the drug into the dog's bloodstream.

Within seconds, the dog slips into un-consciousness and the worker eases him to the floor, speaking softly to him, telling him he is a good dog, stroking and soothing him. In another three to five minutes death is complete. Verification of death is accomplished via an "inter-

cardiac" check, which is the most reliable method. A needle is inserted into the unconscious animal's heart and left there. The syringe moves with the rhythm of the heart, and stops moving when the heart has stopped beating completely.

For cats it is more difficult, and therefore more stressful to the cat, to locate and inject into a vein, so the drug is injected into the abdominal cavity (very young puppies and kittens are also euthanized this way). Although this seems as if it might be painful, a skilled euthanasia technician can perform the injection such that it is virtually unnoticed by the cat. The drug is absorbed into the system slowly, and so the worker holds and pets the cat until he reaches unconsciousness in three to five minutes. He is then gently laid in a dark, quiet cage to minimize stimulus that might interrupt the anesthetic process. Death follows in about thirty minutes. Again, an inter-cardiac check is performed to confirm his heart has stopped beating.

Once death is final, the body is moved to a refrigerated room containing fifty-gallon barrels, which gradually fill with bodies as each day's euthanasia is completed. At the end of two weeks, many of the barrels are full to overflowing, and a renderer arrives to empty them. They are lifted high, tipped, and bodies pour out, spilling into the back of a large truck. The bodies are taken to a rendering plant where, along with roadkill and slaughterhouse scraps, they are processed into bone meal, tallow, proteins and other ingredients used in fertilizers, cosmetics, and, shockingly, even farm animal and pet foods.

The euthanasia process at the shelter in this book is probably as good as the process can be. Many shelters use similar procedures and standards.

Yet every aspect of the process can vary from shelter to shelter. Training requirements vary, and skill levels of individual workers can vary. Not all shelter workers are caring, compassionate animal lovers. The use of pre-euthanasia tranquilizers varies, as do methods of restraining the animals during euthanasia. Some shelters do not use sodium pentobarbital, relying instead on older, inhumane methods of euthanasia like carbon monoxide chambers, or even drowning or gunshots to the head. Those shelters who do use sodium pentobarbital might use it differently. Some do not give abdominal injections to cats and small animals; some inject the drug directly into the heart (which is extremely painful unless the animal is completely anesthetized). Some shelters do not use inter-cardiac verification of death, but instead use a stethoscope, or check for the absence of eye reflexes, or simply wait for rigor mortis.

Body disposal methods also vary. In some communities, bodies are bagged and taken to the local landfill; other shelters cremate them.

Some shelters are not able to, or do not, give attention to an atmosphere of calm. Some euthanize animals in front of other animals. Some shelters euthanize such large numbers of animals that they cannot take individual care with each one, they cannot possibly hold and pet and comfort each animal as he dies. Some shelters euthanize dozens, even a hundred or more, animals every day. Some run eight-hour shifts in which staff do nothing but euthanize animals. The job is horrific, as bad, and probably worse, than you can imagine. While several professions involve dealing with innocent victims, no other profession asks the people in it to kill those they care for, those they came to serve. Most shelter workers are drawn to their profession out of deep love for animals, and the emotional damage they suffer is immense. "There is nothing worse than comforting a scared dog in the morning, then killing that dog in the afternoon," remembers one ex-shelter worker. Many shelters bring in therapists skilled in grief counseling and post traumatic stress syndrome to help staff cope; some operate support groups for staff. The shelter in this book keeps a journal in the euthanasia room for employees to write about, and try to deal with, their grief and pain.

Regardless of shelter procedure and attentiveness to the best possible euthanasia process, a completely humane death is probably not possible. Animals are afraid and confused from the moment they enter a shelter. Some have already been through hell by the time they arrive, their death just the last step of a difficult journey. Being the very sensitive creatures they are, it is likely they know something is wrong prior to their euthanasia – the euthanasia room has a smell and atmosphere which are hard to miss. Some animals are too stressed and agitated for even the most skilled shelter worker to keep the process calm and slow. Some animals are too wild or aggressive to be handled gently, and some animals simply fight it. Euthanasia of these kinds of animals can be difficult and is often less than peaceful. Despite our wish to imagine a gentle and peaceful death to every animal euthanized in a shelter, on a practical level that is just not possible.

Even if a completely, thoroughly humane, death were possible, the critical point is not *how* the animals die, but *that* they die. The way euthanasia is used in this nation's animal shelters is not a true expression of the term: merciful release from intractable suffering. The deaths of millions of animals each year in the animal sheltering system cannot in any way be construed as merciful, as it has more to do with convenience – with society's unwillingness to grapple with ethical solutions to the homeless animal problem – than it does with relief of actual suffering. And while death might be preferable to leaving animals to dangerous, miserable lives on the streets, it should never be considered an adequate answer.

Euthanasia is such an extreme "solution" to the homeless animal problem, that whatever a community's successes – no matter how many adoptions their shelters may do, or how much their euthanasia rate may have decreased – as long as any animal is euthanized for simple lack of a home, it becomes painfully, graphically clear that success is not complete. In this way, the euthanasia that shelters perform acts as an ultimate barometer of success (or failure), a tangible measure of the progress (or lack thereof) that a community has made toward solving its homeless animal problem.

name unknown

This stray female Chow mix was a bundle of nervous energy. She was submissive but distracted, unfocused and jittery. She couldn't handle the overstimulation of the shelter environment and deteriorated quickly, becoming more scared, her energy level nearly frantic. "It's just so stressful in here," sighed a shelter worker.

No one came to claim her, and after four days, the decision was made.

We have made dogs to be our most loyal friends, and they live that role, to the very end. And so they go willingly, with trust. They cooperate when the leash is hooked to their collar, and follow obediently on the last walk they will ever take. She didn't know what would happen to her, but she went. Willingly. With trust... a trust betrayed first by the family who lost her, and then again by a society who can do no better than offer this as their answer.

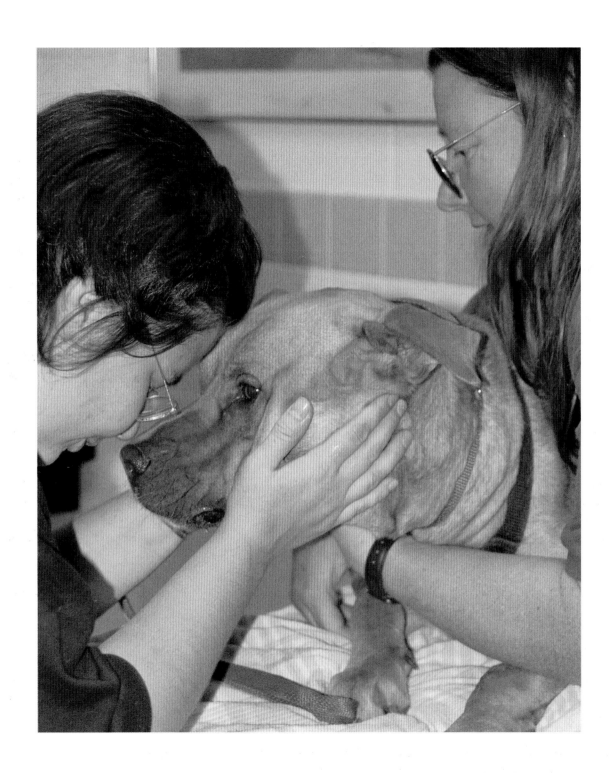

"Good Dog"

From his records: "Has had no training, and uses his weight to get where he wants. Needs to be neutered ASAP, marks his territory non-stop. When he is paying attention to people, he's very loving. Can be overwhelming, jumping up on things and people. Seems very attentive with food and could really do well in a training class."

You see them in shelters all the time: young, healthy male dogs, not neutered, eight to eighteen months old, large, strong, untrained, out of control. Their dispositions are good, they have friendly, even loving, personalities but they're rowdy, they jump on people, they don't know how to walk on a leash, and they have no idea how people want them to behave. Like the juvenile males they are, their hormones are raging and they're distracted by it, less focused on people and more on other dogs, both male and female.

The families that found them irresistible as eight-week old puppies had no idea what they were getting into, not realizing the work and dedication it takes. On the way from cute puppy to big, strong dog, some basic socialization and training was essential, and it didn't happen.

And so the dogs come to shelters in droves, surrendered by their fed-up guardians. Or they arrive as lost animals, also surrendered – indirectly – when nobody comes to look for them.

There is nothing wrong with these dogs, they're just being *dogs*. Just being dogs, however, is not enough. As domesticated animals, we ask them to live compatibly with us in our world, and expect them to behave in certain ways as they move with us through our days. But dogs do not automatically know what is expected of them: they need to be shown and taught. Yet 96% of the dogs surrendered to shelters, according to their guardians, have had absolutely *no* training.

These dogs are not lost causes. Far from it. With consistent positive reinforcement, they would easily learn how they must fit into human culture. Being neutered would calm their hormones and help them to focus better. Given patience and time, love and guidance, they could be wonderful companions and loyal family members.

But it's a common story and there are lots of them. *Lots*. Their behavior makes it difficult for them to attract adopters. Although staff and volunteers consciously try to give these dogs some basic training as they handle them day to day in the shelter, it's just not enough of what these dogs need.

They're not bad dogs, not by a long shot. They're good dogs. Which is exactly what the shelter workers assure them of as their lives are ended.

"Too Old"

"Playing God." This is what shelter workers feel they are doing when they perform the unspeakably difficult task of deciding which animals will be euthanized.

Drawing up the day's euthanasia list – "dispositioning" – involves a multi-dimensional tic-tac-toe of considerations: an individual animal's age, breed, health, and behavior, and how "adoptable" he is because of these things, as well as the overall situation in terms of the numbers and kinds of animals in the shelter, and the ever present question of space availability.

At some point, decisions must be made. Most shelters have guidelines to help, but may also make allowances for subjective judgment and individual circumstances. Some shelters use a committee of staff members to make the decisions; most utilize input from the staff who work directly with the animals.

Shelter workers understand, amongst themselves, the profound horror of deciding who will live and who will die. They know that although a "reason" for euthanasia will be recorded for every animal, most of them are not adequate cause for an animal to die. After all, sick animals could be treated, animals with behavior problems could receive training, scared and shy animals could be comforted, too-young animals could be given time to grow up, old animals could be valued, mixed breed dogs could be as desirable as purebreds. The "reasons" are only symptoms of a shelter system too crowded with animals to ever save them all. Shelter workers know this, and it only makes applying the "reasons" more painful.

The "reason" for these two animals was "too old."

A loving and affectionate orange and white cat was brought to the shelter as a stray. Cataracts covered his eyes and staff estimated his age to be at least ten years. The tri-color Australian Shepherd mix was also a stray, and coincidentally, from the same neighborhood. She seemed distracted and scared, but after some gentle petting grew calm enough to lay her head in a staff person's lap. In the days to follow, she showed herself to be a quiet, well-behaved dog who didn't jump or bark. She, too, was at least ten years old.

Both animals showed all the signs of coming from a home. They were well cared for, social and comfortable around people. It seems incomprehensible that no one came for them. People sometimes harbor the notion that old animals who are missing have "gone off to die somewhere." Perhaps that's what these animals' guardians thought.

What actually happened was much different. The shelter was very full, and cage space was needed. The old cat and old dog had been up for adoption for some time but, because of their age, the chances for either of them were very slim. After a lifetime spent as loving members of their families, these gentle old animals spent their last days in an unfamiliar shelter, and died in the arms of a stranger.

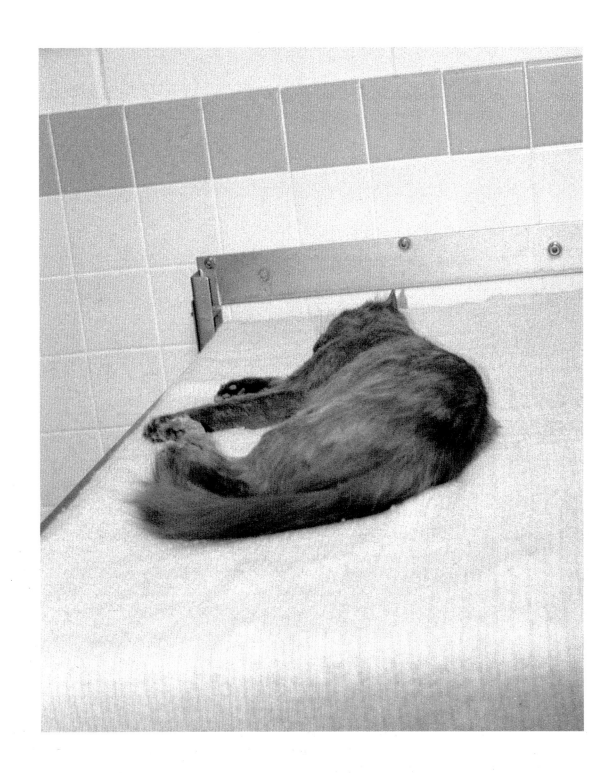

Pearl

Pearl had arrived at the shelter with her newborn kittens over three months before. She did not have an easy time of it. Her shelter records read:

June 18th: Reason for surrender: "Unable to care for."
June 23rd: Kittens have upper respiratory infection, need foster care for two weeks.
June 27th: Christine will foster.
July 22nd: C. brought back from foster today. She also treated for roundworm and coccidia.
July 24th: C. is taking Pearl back to foster for spay and recovery.
August 18th: Pearl has gotten a bit of a cold so she will be in foster a bit longer.
August 26th: Brought back from foster today. Tested negative for feline leukemia and feline immunodeficiency virus at vet. Flea treatment given on the 24th. Personality profile in front office.
August 31st: Treated for tapeworms.
September 14th: Pearl is a special kitty who would do well in a home where the people will let her just be a cat – she's independent, a little aloof. She doesn't like it here and shows her displeasure. From what C. says, she's a great kitty at home, potential adopters should not be put off by her actions here, they should speak with C.
September 16th: Photographed for website.
October 15th: We are FULL. Talked to C. and she understands.

It's a question shelters struggle with every day: how much should an animal be put through to increase her chances for an adoption that may or may not eventually happen?

Pearl was a lovely young cat who had a reasonable chance of being adopted. Providing her with extra medical care seemed like a good bet that could improve her odds of getting a new home – could, in shelter jargon, make her more "adoptable." A healthy cat is more "adoptable." A spayed cat is a more "adoptable." And even setting aside "adoptability" – an absurd category no animal should fall victim to – isn't every animal deserving of basic medical care to improve her health and alleviate her ailments?

It must have been difficult for Pearl: giving birth and nursing her kittens, being abandoned by the people she knew to the stressful shelter, then leaving with strangers to enter another home. She endured trips to the vet, exams, multiple treatments and medications, surgery. It still wasn't over. After all that, she had to return to the shelter again, to live there for weeks, and take her chances at being adopted.

All of what she went through was in her best interest. But she could not know that and shelter life took a toll on her emotional state that she could not hold up to. In the end, all she had endured in the last months of her life was still not enough to secure the one simple thing she needed: someone who would "let her just be a cat."

Charlie

It is a phenomenon so predictable that shelter workers can recite it by heart. Popularized by a movie, or television show, or some other pop culture endeavor, a particular dog breed becomes a "fad." At first, the breed is relatively rare, and that rareness makes it seem exclusive and elite. Soon everyone wants one, has to have it. The breed becomes a status symbol, a fashion statement.

Irresponsible breeders and puppy mills respond, churning out as many of the breed as they can while the demand is high. People buy up the dogs, pleased to have the "coolest" breed. Suddenly, it seems, the dogs are everywhere. Eventually the fad passes, as all fads do, and these same people realize they have acquired a living being with needs, often specialized needs unique to the breed, and find that they weren't prepared for such a commitment. Or they realize they have a dog with health or behavior problems, a common result of breeders and puppy mills who quickly and carelessly produce animals to sell.

Inevitably, shelters end up with the results: kennel after kennel filled with the once-popular dog, now common and therefore less desirable, and so, less adoptable. A short time later, the kennels will be filled with the first of many generations of their mixed-breed offspring.

The fad dog of the 1960's was the Cocker Spaniel. Once considered the quintessential family dog, this breed was gentle, sweet-natured, and tolerant. Overbreeding ruined those characteristics, and many Cockers are now high-strung, unpredictable dogs who are overly shy, sensitive and prone to a behavior named for them: "Cocker Spaniel syndrome," or submissive urination.

It happened with Dalmatians after the wildly successful Disney movie of the mid 1990's. Families rushed to get the "movie" dog their kids fell in love with, not realizing that the Dalmatian, like any breed, has very specific characteristics and needs. Dalmatians are extremely active and require large amounts of exercise. Their temperament is not always a good mix with small children, and they are prone to skin problems that cause massive shedding. Twenty percent of Dalmatians are born deaf in one ear, and another ten to twelve percent are born totally deaf (and the largest organization of Dalmatian breeders in this country strongly recommends "culling" – killing – the deaf puppies). Six months after the movie hit the theaters, Dalmatians began hitting the shelters.

It happened more recently with Chihuahuas, promoted by a national fast food chain's advertising campaign, and with Jack Russell Terriers, popularized by the charmingly intelligent television dog "Eddie." Once relatively uncommon, both breeds are now everywhere, including shelters.

For a period of time in the 1970's, the "fad dog" was the Doberman Pinscher. Originally bred as guard dogs, they are very loyal and devoted to their guardians. They owed their fad popularity to families who wanted "protection," and to those who sought "tough" dogs to enhance their own image. Shelters were, as expected, flooded with Dobermans when the fad faded. As an added disadvantage, movies and television often exaggerated the "protection" image of the breed, portraying them as frightening, irredeemably vicious dogs living in junkyards, or as evil companions to demonic characters. Dobermans are still routinely portrayed this way, and many people have absorbed these images and harbor some fear of the dogs. There are not as many Dobermans or Dobie mixes in shelters now as in the past but they are still very common, the public perception of them lingers, and most often they are just not adopted. Shelter workers receive them with a heavy heart, knowing it is unlikely the dogs will leave alive.

Charlie was a young Doberman who showed the classic beauty and elegance of his breed. His long legs moved gracefully, his brown eyes were deep and soulful. Although his tail had been docked, his ears had been left in their natural, expressive state. ("Ear cropping" is a cosmetic surgery performed on Dobermans and some other breeds like Boxers and Schnauzers. The ears are cut to an unnatural shape and size, then wrapped in tape for weeks to make them stand upright. Many consider this a painful and unnecessary procedure, a disfiguring mutilation that robs a dog of a primary means of communication – the movement of his ears. In fact, it has been banned in many countries, but is still performed routinely in the United Sates. "Tail docking" – amputation of the tail, without anesthesia, within days of a puppy's birth – is another unnecessary cosmetic surgery performed on various breeds.)

Charlie's graceful beauty was complemented by a sweet personality. He was an active, happy dog who liked to please, and shelter records called him "friendly and outgoing." Still, he was a Doberman and no one expressed an interest in adopting him. After three weeks in the shelter, kennel stress began to set in and Charlie started growling and lunging at the dogs in the kennels on either side of him. He barked incessantly, and even a citronella collar, which humanely discourages barking with a distracting fragrant mist, didn't deter him.

Sometimes a break from the shelter environment can stop the progression of kennel stress, at least temporarily, and buy a dog more time for the possibility of adoption. A foster home was located and Charlie had a ten-day respite there, then came back to the shelter. It would undoubtedly be just a matter of time until the kennel stress returned, and shelter staff struggled to find an option for him.

The local Doberman Pinscher rescue group was contacted. Unfortunately, the group rescued only completely purebred Dobermans, which Charlie was not. Breed rescue groups are often as flooded with dogs as shelters, and like shelters, have finite resources that do not allow them to help the too-many animals who need it. This group drew their line at taking in Dobermans who are less than purebred.

The odds were stacked against Charlie in so many ways: a breed that had fallen out of favor; a negative image of his breed that didn't bear any resemblance to his own individual personality; too Doberman to be adopted, but not Doberman enough to be rescued; and a low tolerance for shelter stress... nothing for which this lovely dog was to blame.

Three weeks after his respite in the foster home, he again began to show signs of stress. "This poor guy just cannot handle the stress of being kenneled," his records read. "If we sent him out to foster again, he'd come back to the same thing. We tried."

"Disposition for euthanasia."

Kelli

Kelli, a cute little terrier mix with a heart-stopping face, had been found on a busy highway near the county airport. Her stray hold expired and no one had come forward to claim her, so shelter staff set about getting to know her, to assess her temperament and determine what kind of adoptive family would be best for her. "This poor girl is very frightened but seems sweet. I will continue to spend time with her," noted one of the staffers in her records.

Two days later, the staffer noted, "This pooch has potential, but needs a little work. Quite the little street urchin – wants to be nice but has not learned what affection is all about, will move in close for treats, but is very unsure."

Kelli had no concept of a leash or how to walk alongside a human companion. She craved comfort, wanted to be touched, but was fearful and sometimes skittered away when someone reached to pet her. Shelter staff tried to imagine what had created Kelli's "street urchin" behavior. Was she a "backyard dog" who had received no attention from her family? Had she spent her life on the street, fending for herself? Had she been abused? Had no one ever helped her, showed her that human beings could be kind?

The next day, another staffer noted in her records, "She was really wagging her tail at me today… seems to be improving."

The little ragamuffin dog captured the staff's hearts. Each day they took her out of her kennel to give her basic training and shower her with love. Ten days after entering the shelter, a staffer noted, "Kelli is doing really well, really starting to come around. Very excited to see people and loves to run and play. Very treat-motivated and attentive. Still needs socialization, as she is a bit unsure, but I think she'll do well. Adopters should be prepared to spend some time bonding with her and building her confidence."

Kelli was clearly learning to trust people, to understand what kind of behavior was expected of her, and to enjoy human contact. But the shelter is a stressful place for a frightened dog who lacks confidence, who needs a steady, calm environment in which to develop trust and social skills, who needs time to blossom into her potential of a happy, loving dog.

Staff continued to work with her, and Kelli continued to make progress, but it was a race against time, a race against the onset of kennel stress. A month into her stay at the shelter, she lunged at a small child standing outside her kennel and began to show other signs of stress-induced aggression.

Emotionally, Kelli's time in the shelter must have been very uncomfortable – her newfound, growing trust of humans in conflict with the fear she had lived with for so much longer. Despite the loving, encouraging attention she received, in the stress of the shelter environment her fear finally won out.

Kelly

How much is a life worth?

Kelly was a beautiful golden Husky mix with black sable points and thick, luxuriant fur. She was older, probably at least eight; her eyesight was diminished and she was beginning to show hip problems.

The animal control officer arriving at work at 6 a.m. discovered her in the shelter's play yard. Probably someone had found her on their way to work, brought her to the shelter and finding it not yet open, left her in the yard.

Her guardian was contacted using the information on the tag she was wearing and came to get her a few hours later. She seemed relieved to know Kelly was safe, but upon learning that she would be required to pay a standard twenty dollar reclaim fee, she balked. "Why would I pay when she'll only get out again?" asked the woman. Apparently Kelly had been lost before.

After arguing with the staff over the fee, she decided she was unwilling to pay it, and instead began the paperwork that would sign Kelly over to the shelter. "She'll get adopted, won't she? She's a great dog!" she said. The staff made it clear that there were no guarantees and that not all animals surrendered to the shelter got new homes.

Still, the woman continued with the paperwork, even filling out a personality profile documenting Kelly's life and history: she had been "adopted from a family" by this woman two years ago and had at one point been trained to assist a visually impaired person. In her current home, though, she was primarily a "yard dog," sleeping in a doghouse and being fed outside in the mornings. The woman wrote that Kelly was "extremely loving and lovable, very well-behaved, gets along with children, elderly and other pets; will walk well with you on a leash as well as take you for daily runs; a good companion."

Nonetheless, she completed the paperwork and walked out, keeping her twenty dollars in exchange for Kelly.

The staff was dumbfounded. If Kelly was such a "great, loving" dog, why would her guardian give her up over twenty dollars? Had she been looking for an excuse to get rid of the dog? Did she actually want to find her a new home? Knowing Kelly might not be adopted, how could the woman leave her there? There was simply no rational explanation, and sadly, it wasn't the first time, nor would it be the last, that shelter staff witnessed such inexplicable behavior.

Back in the kennels, Kelly was devastated. Her grief was unmistakable. She did not eat, would not look up at anyone who stood in front of her kennel, did not lift her head as her photo was taken. She was so unresponsive, staff even wondered if she might be deaf. After three days, it was clear she was not going to bounce back from the trauma of being abandoned; puppies, even street dogs, do better in the shelter, having never known a home. It is the ones who had a home – the ones who have lost the most – who suffer the worst. And Kelly suffered immensely.

Her very suffering sealed her fate, virtually guaranteeing that she would not be adopted. An older dog, deeply depressed, would need the rarest, most sensitive of adopters to notice her, to consider taking her on.

These are the cases that make shelter workers turn hopeless, depressed, angry, bitter. These are the cases that make them feel that their shelter is not, as they wish, sanctuary and safety for animals, but instead, an institution that makes easy the disposal of living beings. These are the cases that make them feel that their job is cleaning up after a society that doesn't care.

They were angry and sad at Kelly's situation. But they put it aside, choked it back, and focused on giving Kelly tenderness and dignity as they eased her from this world, as the priceless life that was Kelly slipped away.

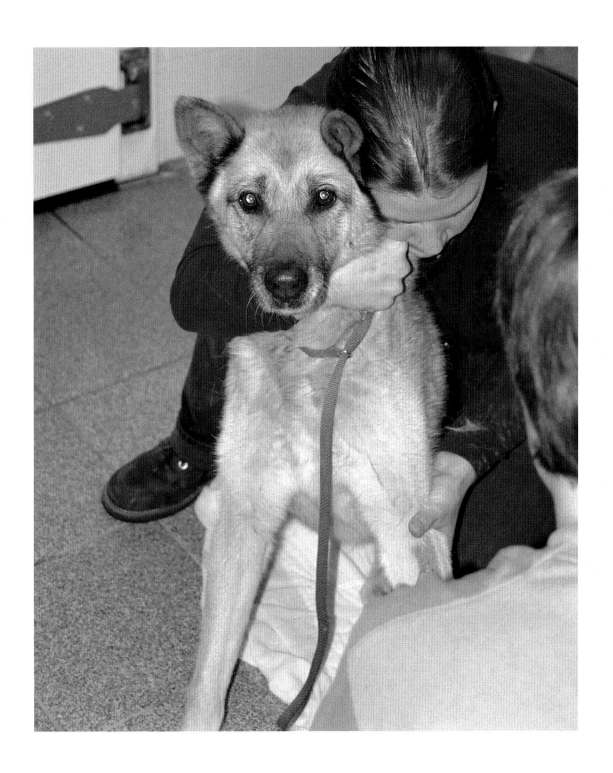

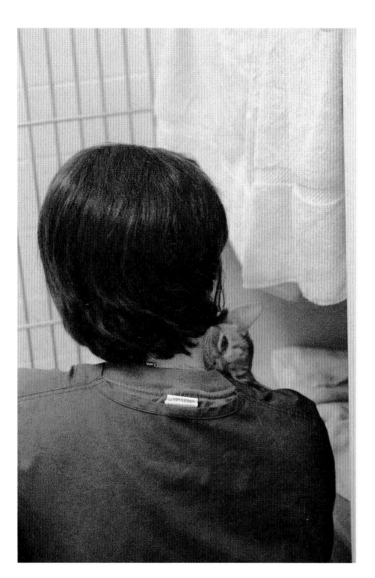

six cats

Six cats. Each a unique individual. Each with a story, a past, a life.

Three were surrendered by their guardians. Three were strays. In the end, all were unwanted. Like the millions of others, nowhere to go, no one to step up for them.

On this day, six living beings became numbers on a euthanasia list.

one week

At the beginning of the week, the barrels in the refrigerated room were empty. Seven days later, two were overflowing with the remains of unwanted lives.

From the staff journal in the shelter euthanasia room:

"Go to a better place."

Chapter 5

THERE'S NO PLACE LIKE HOME

"Home." Such a small, simple word, but in a shelter, there is no more powerful idea. Home is the ever-present thought, the all-encompassing goal; it hangs in the air and occupies everyone's minds. In a shelter, the search for a home is *everything* – for every lost cat whose stray hold has expired without being claimed, for every puppy and kitten born into an already overpopulated world, for every dog given up by his guardian, *home* is now the ultimate hope, the slender thread by which his fate hangs, the magic wish that will mean the difference between life and death.

Nationally, however, only 20% of the dogs and cats in homes are adopted from animal shelters. Though solutions to the homeless animal problem must focus on preventing animals from even being in shelters in the first place, the low percentage of animals obtained from shelters certainly compounds the tragedy.

Shelters struggle to get the word out that their facilities are filled to overflowing with beautiful, loving dogs and cats who are eager to become loyal companions to new guardians. Most do everything they can to promote adoptions and put their animals in the public eye, by showing them on television, in newspapers, and at community events. Some showcase animals in pet supply stores or set up off-site adoptions in storefronts or mobile adoption vans. Many have websites listing animals who need homes. Others maintain waiting lists for particular types or breeds of animals so they can alert interested people when those animals are available at the shelter.

Some shelters put together appealing adoption packages including helpful items like a collar and ID tag or microchip, leash or cat carrier, vaccinations, free veterinary exam, spay or neuter surgery, training classes, information packets, and even treats and toys.

Within the shelter, staff and volunteers work to show the animals to their best advantage. Some flag cages with bright "adoptable" signs and post personalized information about each animal. Some bathe and groom animals to look their best (and being fresh and clean seems to increase the animals' confidence as well). And they strive always to reduce stress, so that adopters can see the animals' true spirits of joy and happiness.

Those generous people who adopt from a shelter grant the ultimate wish, literally giving the gift of life to an animal who needs a second chance. And some believe that the animals are quite aware of this. Many adopters will tell you that the animals seem to *know* they have been saved and are *grateful,* doing everything they can to fit into their new family and becoming extremely devoted to their new guardians.

Whether they are aware of their predicament is something we may never know, but we do know this: a shelter animal can, given the chance, bring untold joy and love to a new family who loves him back. He will give the gifts of friendship and devotion, and will give them unconditionally. He'll share his own unique spirit and teach his own unique lessons. He will help us remember our connection to other living beings, and show us the way to making that connection loving and respectful.

Honoring these things by adopting a homeless animal is a profound act, an expression of compassion and of the inherent value of animals, a stand for life and against meaningless death. Most importantly, and most basically, it is the happy ending to a shelter animal's story... a *home.*

Pancha

Pancha's photo captures her perfectly: an exuberant, out-going dog who loves people, she greeted everyone with a happy "in your face" enthusiasm.

Like all animals, she deserved a home that she could count on for the rest of her life, to be protected, cared for, and cherished. In return, she would joyfully give boundless, unconditional love. The family who wanted to adopt her would have a lot to consider if they were to be able to fulfill their end of that wonderful bargain.

The adoption process intends to help an adopter through those considerations: the everyday care and attention an animal needs, as well as the unexpected and difficult life events that can, and do, happen to both animal and family. The shelter wants to help the adopter understand what it means to take on an animal, and what it means to have that intangible quality – *commitment* – that will make an adoption last a lifetime.

Each shelter has its own adoption process and its own criteria for approving an adoption. Most have some kind of application or questionnaire, and most require an interview with a staff person. Some require written landlord approval if the adopter is a renter. Some require fenced yards for dogs, or that cats be indoor-only. Many ask all members of the family to participate, so that everyone is involved in this important decision.

The adoption process makes some people feel that they are being "grilled" or "put through the ringer" to get an animal, but the concern behind the process is well-founded. Shelters are all too familiar with the myriad ways in which the human-animal bond can break, and each part of the process intends to prevent a specific problem that could cause an adoption to fail. A shelter animal who is lucky enough to be adopted has already beaten the odds once; shelters want to do all they can to ensure the animal is finally and *permanently* safe, and never again has to take her chances in a shelter or on the streets, *ever*.

As it turned out, Pancha had heartworm, a deadly disease requiring a long and expensive treatment. She was also difficult to contain – although happy in her new home, she broke out of the yard and traveled the neighborhood several times. Both of these developments were unexpected and challenging, but Pancha's family had made a commitment to her when they adopted her and they expressed that commitment with their actions. They took on the time and expense of the medical treatment she needed, and they worked with patience and perseverance to finally thwart her creative escape efforts.

Odds are there will be other challenges in their life together. Some are predictable; others will come unexpectedly. And while no one can be totally prepared for everything that might happen, it becomes a responsibility to anticipate as much as possible. An animal, after all, will have no choice but to depend upon her guardian to get them both safely through life's uncertainties.

Bogie

Bogie was a dog with a big heart beating in a pit bull body. A stray who arrived at the shelter wearing a brown leather collar and a flea collar, he was sweet, affectionate, and loving, but he was not claimed by his guardian.

Pit bulls have come to be seen as a scourge of our modern day urban society. Frightening news stories tell of horrific incidents involving pit bulls, and leave us feeling that the dogs are loaded weapons, nightmares waiting to happen. Communities across the country have responded, passing ordinances that attempt to ban the very existence of pit bulls from their homes and their streets. There is much debate, however, as to whether such breed-specific "vicious dog" legislation is enforceable or even effective, as determining a dog's breed is often a subjective judgment, and the people who want aggressive dogs are quite willing to move their focus to other, still-legal breeds like Rottweilers and German Shepherds.

"Pit bull" is actually a general term for three different dog breeds, the American Staffordshire Terrier, the American Bulldog, and the American Pit Bull Terrier. As a whole, these breeds are physically very strong, intelligent, active, very trainable and responsive to their guardians with a desire to please. Although all purebred dogs and cats are manipulated by humans to create specific physical and psychological traits, the pit bull is the victim of the worst kind of manipulation. Playing on their natural characteristics, the dogs have been bred for over a century to fight, to maim, to kill and be killed, for human entertainment.

In a dog fight, two dogs are placed together in a "pit" – a small arena enclosed by plywood walls – to fight each other until one is unable or unwilling to continue. A fight can last an hour or more. The injuries suffered by the animals are severe, and the dogs often die from shock, blood loss, exhaustion, and infection. Dogs who lose are brutally punished or killed by their "owners," or just abandoned, no longer wanted. Other animals are also victimized in this wretched activity. Fighting dogs are trained using "bait" animals like rabbits, cats, or small dogs. Children are often present at dog fights, where they undoubtedly absorb attitudes of violence and are desensitized to the suffering of other living beings.

Despite the fact that dog fighting is illegal in every state, and is a felony in most, this horrific activity still takes place with sickening regularity and is far from being stopped. It occurs in both impoverished rural areas as well as inner cities, and can be a lucrative activity for the humans involved, as spectators pay admission to the fights, and may gamble thousands of dollars on the outcomes.

Shelters began seeing an influx of pit bulls and pit bull mixes over a decade ago. The influx has grown to near epidemic proportions in some shelters, especially those in large cities and urban areas. In a shelter system already too overwhelmed to adequately help every animal, pit bulls, with their heavy baggage stand almost no chance.

Virtually all shelters have handled pit bulls with a simple yet sweeping policy: *absolutely no adoptions*. Any unclaimed or surrendered dog who appears to be one of the pit bull breeds, or even a mixed breed dog with a large proportion of pit bull, is taken straight to the euthanasia room. Shelters have felt that it is irresponsible, to say nothing of an enormous liability risk, to place any potentially dangerous dog in a home. It is also a very real fact that some of the people who are interested in adopting pit bulls are interested for all the wrong reasons, a motivation not willingly revealed during the adoption process.

Pit bull advocates maintain that pit bulls are not naturally aggressive toward humans since they have been selectively bred to enhance their aggression toward other dogs. In fact, they say, pit bulls who are aggressive toward people are made that way through severe lack of socialization, and the "training" for fighting that includes punishment, mistreatment and extreme abuse.

In recent years, some shelters have re-examined their policies regarding these dogs, and have taken the position that not every pit bull is destined to be dangerous. More and more shelters are becoming skilled in the techniques of canine temperament testing, which allows them to assess a dog's *individual* personality to determine his suitability for adoption.

A temperament test puts a dog through a series of controlled situations and measures his responses to gauge various characteristics of his personality: tolerance for confinement and isolation; sociability and past socialization; trainability and prior training; responsiveness to other animals; levels of dominance, tolerance, excitability and energy; and overall psychological stability. An assessment of any dog's temperament is critically valuable information in making a good match between dog and new home. For a pit bull, the information can be life-saving: a dog once condemned solely on the basis of his breed can now be treated as the individual he is.

Shelters who are "pit bull friendly" are nonetheless extremely careful about the adoptions. The potential for fighting has been written into the dogs' genetics, and though a pit bull may never express the slightest bit of aggression, shelters still look for a knowledgeable and dedicated guardian who will understand and avoid situations that could trigger fighting behavior. In today's climate, a pit bull will be blamed for any incident with a human or other animal, whether or not he actually instigated it, and even if he was provoked or defending himself. A pit bull is also at greater risk than usual should he become lost – many people will be too scared to approach him or help him. An educated, careful guardian is essential to a pit bull's long term safety.

Bogie was tested and found to have a responsive, tolerant, and stable temperament. His exuberant personality attracted several potential adopters, and after a number of people expressed interest in him, the right adopter appeared.

Before he could go to his new home, the shelter arranged for a veterinarian to neuter Bogie and implant microchip identification. The shelter also required that Bogie and his new guardian attend training classes together, and that his guardian post a monetary deposit which would be refunded when the classes were completed.

Blessed with knowledgeable and careful adoption practices, Bogie got a second chance. He was saved by an adopter, and a shelter, who saw beyond his pit bull body, who saw his loving spirit, and who saw him as an individual.

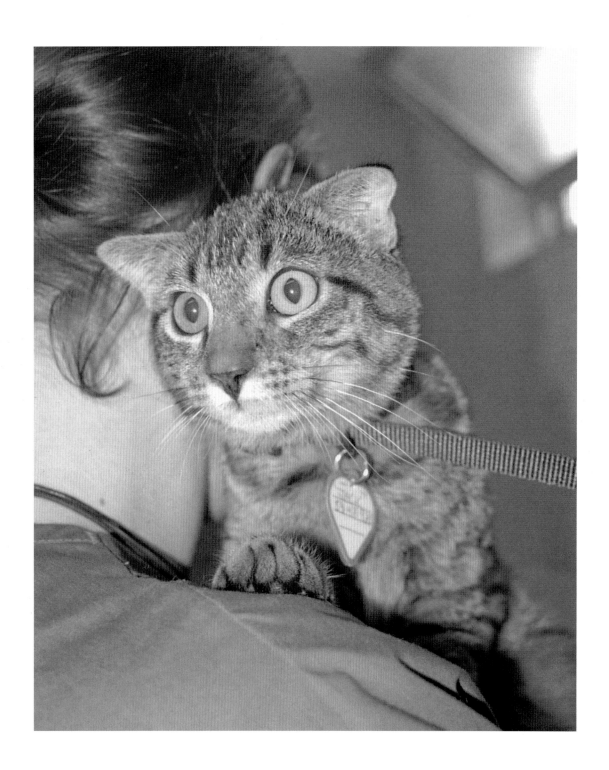

Jack

"We want to adopt the one who needs it the most," the couple said when they entered the shelter.

A generous and compassionate intent, but not such an easy choice. In a very real way, *all* the animals in the shelter "need it the most." How do you choose? The one who has been there the longest? The one who is becoming depressed? The one who is oldest? The one who is sick or injured? The one whose very plain coloring or markings make it less likely that he will attract an adopter? The run-of-the-mill, common stray at risk simply because he and his story *are* so common?

As they walked through the kennels, wanting to do the right thing, they were almost overwhelmed with opportunities. Eventually they found Jack, a six month old Scottish Fold mix cat who had been surrendered to the shelter by his previous guardian.

"There's something about his eyes," they said when they came to his cage. After meeting and spending some time with him, learning what they could of his brief background, they decided he was the one they would choose, the one who would go home with them.

So many animals. They all, each and every one of them, deserve to be chosen, and so you pick one who is a good match for you, and one who moves you. And because they are all at risk, no matter who you pick, you are saving a life.

She Devil

One of the more artful aspects of adoptions is making good matches between animals and people. It is not as simple as finding a dog who grabs the heart, or being captivated by an adorable kitten. Each animal has her own unique personality, but also carries traits inherited from the breeds of her parents, traits which can make her more, or less, compatible with various types of homes and families.

Border Collies and Australian Shepherds, for instance, are "working" dogs, bred to herd. By nature they are active and need to be busy. Left alone for long periods of time they can become bored and destructive, so are often not good matches for working families who are gone all day. Sight hounds, the family of dogs that include Greyhounds and Whippets, are bred to respond to movement and have a tendency to chase cats. Afghans' and Persians' long coats need extensive grooming, which can be too labor intensive for a busy family. Purebred animals have a higher incidence of health problems and genetic defects, since breeding for appearance defies natural selection, which would choose characteristics for survival of the fittest rather than aesthetics. Cocker Spaniels, for instance, are prone to ear infections, Himalayan cats tend to have respiratory problems and many German Shepherds are afflicted with hip dysplasia. These health problems can mean a commitment to more veterinary care than other animals may need.

She Devil was a barely-eight week old Rhodesian Ridgeback puppy, found abandoned in a box in front of a local utility office. Ridgebacks are *big* dogs with a high energy level. Combined with their strongly independent and even stubborn personalities, good training is essential to be able to control them to ensure their safety.

She Devil was already a textbook example of the most challenging attributes of her breed. Despite being small enough to lift with one hand, she seemed to fill her kennel, as if she already had all the energy required to operate the huge body she would one day grow into. She definitely needed a family who would understand her distinct personality and be willing to work with it.

But She Devil charmed everyone who saw her. She was exuberant and bossy, practically commanding anyone who stood in front of her kennel to take her home with them. Adopters who came in to consider small dogs, or mixed breed dogs, or adult dogs, fell under her spell and wanted her, despite being wholly unprepared for the commitment she would require.

Sometimes adoption counseling involves talking people *out* of certain animals. The goal of the shelter is not to find *any* home, but a *permanent* home, and that means a match based on a rational, well-informed choice. While She Devil worked on seducing all passers-by, shelter staff worked on finding the right home. A week after arriving at the shelter, a family affiliated with the local Rhodesian Ridgeback rescue group adopted her. Their knowledge, understanding, and experience provided the solid foundation upon which She Devil's new home could be built – a home that would last a lifetime.

name unknown

Many people want a puppy or kitten as a new companion, and it's not hard to understand why, but there is something very special about adopting an older animal. These often-overlooked animals offer unique qualities that only age and maturity can provide.

Older animals are past the destructive phases of their youth. Those who have had a puppy or kitten know that they are capable of chewing, climbing, shredding and destroying in amazingly creative ways that are hard to anticipate. Life with an older animal is calmer, more peaceful, and less labor intensive.

Older animals are less rambunctious, more focused, patient and gentle. They can actually be *better* with small children than puppies and kittens and can be an easier addition to a busy family. They are very good matches for adults who have less active lives or seniors who aren't equipped to handle the activity levels and needs of young animals.

The older animal has already become the size and shape he was meant to be, so "what you see is what you get" – and you will know exactly what that is. Older animals may come with the benefit of information from a previous guardian on the animal's history, health, habits, likes and dislikes. And although all animals need a post-adoption adjustment period, older animals who have been in a home may already be familiar with household routines and understand how to fit in.

This fluffy orange and white cat was a stray who had gone unclaimed by his family. "This incredibly sweet boy looks well cared for. Older, neutered. Super purr!" noted staff in his records.

He was not a playful kitten who would entertain a new guardian with high-energy antics. He *was* a ready-made lap cat, which is exactly what he showed the older woman who came to the shelter to adopt a companion. Flopping on the floor in the "get-acquainted room," he gazed up at her and kneaded his paws in the air, as if to show her how relaxed and affectionate he would be in her home, what a lovely companion he could be for her.

She gazed back at him and saw a good match, and decided to take him home. In doing so, she granted the gift of life to an older animal who was at a distinct disadvantage for getting a second chance. She made a poignant commitment to a sweet, old cat who needed and deserved someone – someone like her – who would look beyond his years to see his loving being.

Bree

Feral dogs are a growing problem in this country; they comprise a largely undocumented and unstudied population. In the decaying urban areas of many large cities, thousands and thousands of these dogs live in abandoned warehouses and buildings, under bridges, in empty lots and city woods. Starving, they roam the streets in packs in search of food and shelter.

They are the stray "guard" dogs and fighting dogs who have been abandoned and left to their own devices to survive. The combination of their genetics – purposeful breeding for aggression – and the fighting, abuse, and lack of socialization in their backgrounds can make them dangerous animals. The feral offspring born to these strays are terrified of humans, hiding and avoiding contact, almost like their wild wolf ancestors. But unlike their wild relatives, their domestication over tens of thousands of years has left them without survival skills.

In many cities in the United States, the feral dog problem has become epidemic. These dogs suffer immensely from starvation, disease, injury, and lack of shelter. They are subject to horrible abuse and very few people or organizations dedicate themselves to helping or defending them. Despite the fact that they are victims – of the humans who created their situations and of their own genetics – there is little compassion for them.

A woman called the animal control officers to come pick up the little gray and white cattle dog. The dog was running with a pack of stray dogs, and although the pack was thought to be feral, the cattle dog clearly was not: she had been entering the woman's house through the cat door to steal food. The little dog knew a house meant food, and she was very resourceful, or desperate, to get it.

The animal control officer who picked her up thought the dog had little or no socialization. Whether that was true, or whether she became that way from being on her own and taking care of herself or from living with the dog pack, no one could guess. But after just a few days in the shelter, a different personality began to emerge. She was friendly, greeting visitors enthusiastically, wagging her tail and maneuvering her body at the front of her kennel to ask for petting and scratching. "She has come around tons since she got here, I think she has a chance," noted a shelter worker in her file.

Just five days after arriving, a woman fell for her, hard. "I already love her," she said after meeting her, "and I already know that her name will be Bree."

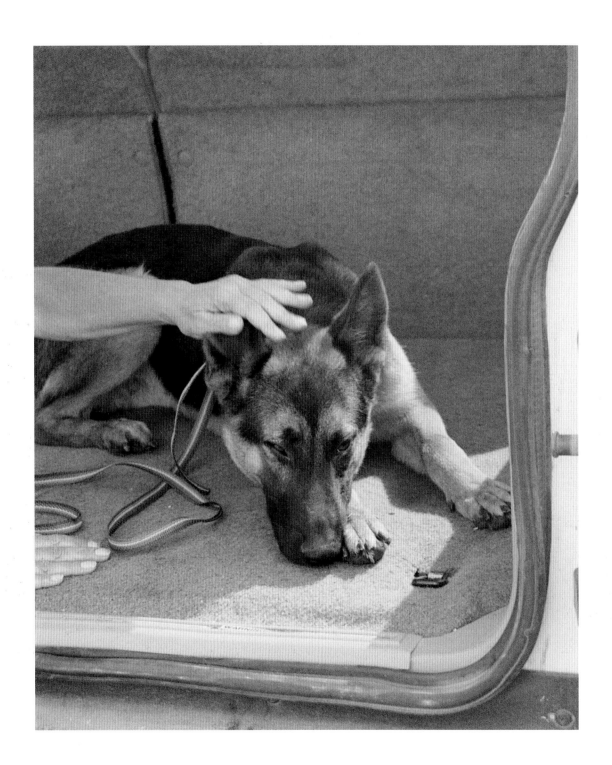

Lykos

For many people, deciding which animal to adopt is a difficult, if not agonizing, experience. But for others, it is something close to magic....

A person comes to the shelter, walks up and down the aisles of kennels, gazing into the eager eyes of the animals. Amongst all the others, a certain face stands out. A certain dog or cat draws the person back. What is that special, unexpected connection that happens between an animal and a human? What do they see in each other? Most people can't explain it, except to say that something just *clicks* and suddenly they know this is the animal for them.

Lykos was a graceful German Shepherd who was found darting through busy traffic, lost, confused and frightened. Two days after he arrived at the shelter, a soft-spoken woman visited, to consider adopting a dog. She looked at Lykos, he looked back, and in that moment, it *clicked* – their bond was formed.

The woman immediately spoke with shelter staff and told them that if Lykos hadn't been claimed by the end of his stray hold period, she would adopt him. And indeed, the soft-spoken woman returned to the shelter, to wait as the clock ticked down and the stray hold expired. Knowing that "love at first sight" isn't enough, she spent time learning what little was known about Lykos' background, his breed, and what the staff had observed about his personality. She completed the adoption application and interview, and it was clear she was prepared, committed, and ready to take Lykos into her home and her life... he had already found his way into her heart. The papers were signed, and Lykos hopped into her car.

Trying to explain something almost unexplainable, she said simply, "I loved him the minute I saw him."

Sandy & Willy

It could have been the typical shelter story: too many animals to give all of them what they need. The animals with additional, special needs, face an uphill battle to survive. Those with extraordinary needs have the odds stacked extraordinarily against them.

But not this time. Sometimes, despite the overwhelming odds, there can be exceptions to the rules. Although it shouldn't take a miracle for a homeless animal to get what he needs, it often takes something close, and sometimes, with a little help from friends, miracles do happen.

Sandy, a neutered Golden Retriever mix, was found stray. The veterinarian who volunteered at the shelter examined Sandy, found cataracts on his eyes, very worn teeth, and estimated Sandy to be at least nine or ten years old. Worse, the veterinarian discovered a tumor on Sandy's spleen, which explained the dog's thinness and overall depleted health. Spleen tumors are usually benign but must be removed, and the surgery to do so is quite expensive.

Sandy's shelter records noted he "plays ball non-stop," and that he was "lovely, gentle, and responsive; this dog would be great for a first-time guardian, seems like a real easy keeper aside from the medical issues." A number of people considered adopting Sandy, but, as his file noted, "for interested people the price to fix this boy up is going to be over $1,400."

An old dog in a crowded shelter, with health problems and an expensive medical bill... it's not hard to imagine the end of this story. But Sandy's story was not going to have a typical ending. One by one, people stepped in to help. Piece by piece, the arrangements fell into place for Sandy to get the medical treatment he needed. A local animal rescue group found a veterinarian who agreed to perform the surgery at no cost, a volunteer offered to provide transportation to and from the veterinary clinic, a foster home offered to care for Sandy during his long recuperation.

Finally, the surgery took place. The veterinarian removed a very large tumor, which turned out to be benign.

A potential adopter who had been following Sandy's story went to the foster home to meet him, fell in love, and after completing the adoption process at the shelter, took Sandy home.

Meanwhile, Willy, a black Lab-Chow mix, was running loose on a busy street and was hit by a car. A concerned citizen transported him to the nearest veterinarian, who stabilized him and put a temporary cast on his badly-broken front leg. Willy was wearing a cat tag with a registration code and a toll-free phone number, but when called, the service had no record of the tag ever being registered.

Once he was stabilized, Willy was transferred from the veterinary clinic to the shelter. The diagnosis, however, was not good. X-rays showed that Willy would need surgery to insert a metal plate in his leg to repair the break. It was a difficult, and expensive, procedure.

Shelter staff worried about Willy and whether they would be able to provide what he needed. A staffer who worked with Willy found him to be a "good boy," but thought his background might have included some abuse. When she told him to "sit," or when she attempted to brush him, Willy became frightened and cowered on the ground, trying to scurry away. Despite his fear, and despite the trauma he had just been through, she noted that Willy was "incredibly sweet," tolerating the bear hugs she showered on him, and eventually enjoying being brushed. He was good on a leash, never barked, and was friendly toward cats and other dogs. "I think this dog would become a great loving companion, and I hope he gets his leg fixed because then he will truly be able to run around and be a happy dog," she wrote.

The veterinarian who took Willy's x-rays offered his help to find an orthopedic specialist who might be willing to donate some of the expense of the surgery. But even with such a donation, he feared it would cost over a thousand dollars. In the meantime, he replaced the cast, inserting a splint to keep Willy's leg stable. Willy clunked around his kennel on the cast, remaining amazingly good-natured and happy.

At last, the veterinarian found a specialist who would help by performing the surgery for a very reduced cost. It would be paid for by the shelter's "Second Chance Fund," a special reserve created to pay for out-of-the-ordinary medical treatment needed by individual animals due to injury, illness, or abuse. Many shelters maintain these types of reserves, calling them by a variety of names like "Cinderella Funds" or "Rags to Riches Funds." The funds are supported by caring donors whose contributions enable a shelter to provide the exceptional treatment that can help an animal make the transformation from one with serious medical problems, to one who is ready for a new home.

Thanks to the generous Second Chance Fund donors, and to the compassionate veterinarians, Willy had the surgery to repair his leg. The foster family who helped Sandy during his recovery offered to help once again, and Willy recuperated under their loving care.

The woman who adopted Sandy had also met Willy at the shelter, and upon hearing Willy's story, decided that she wanted to adopt *him* too. Now Sandy and Willy are both able to "run around and be happy dogs" in the same home.

Shelters can't do it all by themselves. But when caring members of a community – volunteers, concerned citizens, other animal rescue groups, veterinarians, adopters, donors – come together, each stepping forward to offer their bit of help, their actions combine to save lives. The cases that seem hopeless instead gather their own momentum and beat the odds. Sandy and Willy's "happy ending" shows us how it *should* be, for all animals, while offering us a vision of how it *can* be, when people get involved and let compassion be their guide.

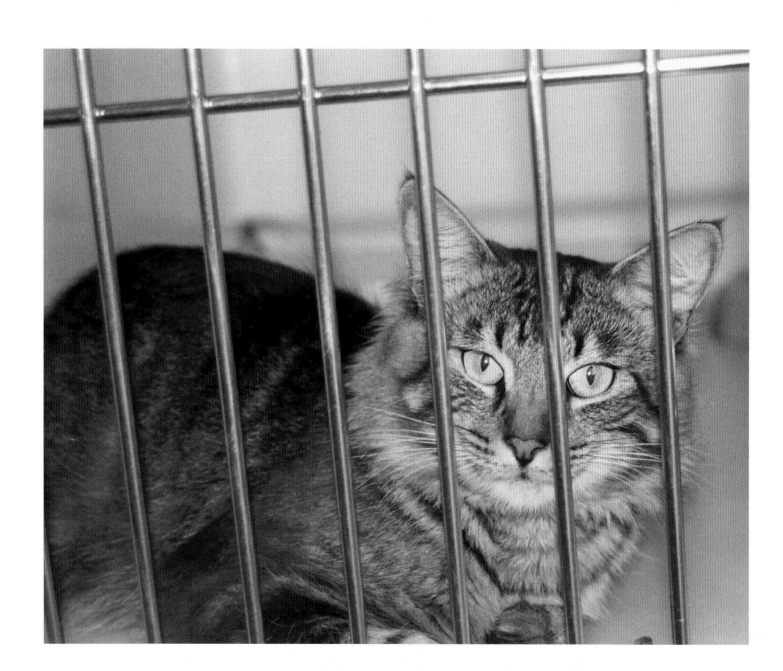

Pablo

Pablo, a stray brown tabby, and the recipient of every possible effort to get him adopted, was the animal who had been at the shelter the longest – nearly four months. He was that rare cat who seemed unfazed by long confinement in a cage. He started out as a friendly, outgoing cat and remained so throughout the long weeks and months, showing no signs of kennel stress. He became a favorite of staff and volunteers, the front of his cage overflowing with comment cards from those who had spent time with him, proclaiming his virtues and begging potential adopters to consider him: "So very, very sweet!" "Handsome, affectionate." "Truly a people-cat." "Playful, patient, kind and gentle." "*Please* adopt him – he is such a sweetheart!"

Still, Pablo seemed to be as unlucky as his stay was long. Time after time, he was passed over, and when the cat kennels were completely full and cage space was needed, Pablo was an obvious candidate for euthanasia. The decision was made, but when another staff member pleaded for just a bit more time, the supervisor gave Pablo a reprieve, knowing that it couldn't be for long.

Just two days later, Pablo's luck changed. A woman came to the shelter looking for a new feline companion. She was intent on making a good match, proceeding thoughtfully through the adoption process with a staff person. She had already spent time with several cats by the time she met Pablo. The staffer brought Pablo to meet her and was horrified when Pablo "acted like a lunatic and jumped on the woman's head." Heart sinking, the staffer assumed that Pablo had just ruined his last chance to get out of the shelter alive.

But Pablo's luck was running strong... the adopter fell in love with him, no matter that he might be a "lunatic," and wanted to give him a home. She had no idea – the staffer did not tell her – how very close to the end Pablo was. Although every shelter adoption is nothing short of a life-saving event, Pablo's was an especially vivid example, and an especially magical happy ending.

Duke & Lady

Dogs, more than any other companion animals, are shaped by their circumstances and the environment in which they live, the world we provide for them. Although each has a unique breed, personality and spirit, our decisions for them play a large part in determining who they will become.

Often, animals kept as "working dogs" – herding dogs, racing dogs, and sledding dogs, for instance – are perceived as having a "job" to do and are not considered family members. Duke and Lady, two gorgeous Blue Tick Coon Hounds, a breed commonly used for hunting, had spent their entire lives chained to their dog houses.

All dogs, even so-called working dogs, are social creatures who crave the company of their pack – other dogs and human beings. Deprived of social contact, dogs who live on chains exist in a constant state of boredom and frustration from "watching the world go by."

Chained dogs also live in a state of continual physical discomfort – they are forced to eat and sleep in the same confined area in which they defecate and urinate. The area is usually dirt or mud, any grass worn away by their pacing. They are subject to the extremes of heat and cold. Their necks chafe from the constant pulling and rubbing of their collars, and they risk choking or hanging should their chain get tangled. Most receive poor care, in an "out of sight, out of mind" relationship with their guardians. They are the potential victims of cruelty by people or attack by other animals, for they cannot escape danger.

Animal behavior experts agree that constant chaining is not good for a dog. In fact, it is one of the most psychologically damaging conditions in which a dog can be kept. The psychological stress, coupled with the physical discomfort, creates dogs who are neurotic, anxious, and even aggressive. Some communities have acknowledged that chaining is so cruel and such an inadequate method of caring for a dog that they have enacted ordinances prohibiting it.

A concerned neighbor reported Duke and Lady's living situation to the shelter. An animal control officer investigated and talked to their guardian as to why the conditions in which the dogs were being kept were not adequate. The officer had the authority to issue citations, confiscate the animals, and charge the dogs' guardian with animal cruelty. But, rather than correcting the inadequate conditions, the guardian surrendered the dogs to the shelter, agreeing to not acquire any more in the future.

As expected, Duke and Lady were heartbreaking examples of why dogs cannot be kept chained. Their psychological damage was severe and obvious. Completely unsocialized and unaccustomed to any human contact, they were terrified of everyone and everything. They cowered and whined. They growled when approached, although, amazingly, they would not bite. They knew nothing of the pleasure of being petted, and tried desperately to get away from the slightest physical touch. Noises made them nervous, and they were confused by the freedom of being let off a leash to move where they wanted. They were overwhelmed by just being out in the world.

They were simply *not* candidates for adoption, they were far too damaged.

But the animal control officer could not forget them, and despite the dogs' severe problems, she decided to adopt them herself. She had the experience and expertise to handle dogs with such severe problems, but it was still a huge commitment. Duke and Lady would probably never completely heal psychologically, and would almost certainly never be typical dog companions. They would need special care all of their lives to keep them safe and to give them whatever happiness they might be able to salvage.

As the officer began to live with Duke and Lady and care for them, she found that they were intimidated even by positive experiences, by rewards and treats and kindness. She stuck with them, being careful not to push them too quickly, meeting them with constant love and gentleness. And as she did, they slowly began to be comfortable with her – to turn to her for reassurance when they were nervous and for safety when they were scared. Slowly, they began to bond with her, and slowly, she showed them the world... a world filled with the good things of dog life, a world where they were loved and respected.

Now, after many, *many* months of patient, persistent kindness and loving care, Duke and Lady are calmer and more cautiously happy than anyone predicted they could ever be. The dogs live a sheltered life, dictated by what they can handle and what makes them happy. Both continue to be frightened of strangers and strange places, and probably always will be. Lady, especially, remains very timid. She has good days, when she has the confidence to greet people, and bad days, when she can't come out from under the desk where she hides.

But they have discovered their hounds' noses, the joy of smell that is in a scent hound's blood. They revel in each other's company, and play and romp together. They've learned the simple, luxurious pleasure of sleeping on a soft couch. And, with their new guardian in their new home, they have found a measure of well-deserved peace.

Madison

Madison's adoption was what every adoption should be.

An older, less active dog, Madison was selected by an older, less active couple who instinctively knew that the first step in a successful adoption was choosing an animal who was likely to match their lifestyle. They met Madison and played with her in the shelter's "get acquainted" yard. The couple had never had a dog, and so they availed themselves of the knowledge and expertise of shelter staff. They talked with an adoption counselor for a long while about the basics of canine care: exercise, food, veterinary care; as well as the subtleties of giving a dog a happy life: loving attention and consistent routine, happy play and warm comfort.

The couple went home to think about it overnight.

The next day they returned, to spend more time getting to know Madison and to ask follow-up questions of the staff. Then they left again, to consider the commitment they were making, and to do so in a neutral environment away from the emotionally-charged atmosphere of the shelter. They would return by four o'clock, they said, if they decided to adopt Madison.

At five minutes to four, they were back, certain that they wanted to take Madison home, ready to make the adjustments necessary to bring a dog into their family, committed to providing for Madison for the rest of her life. It was a careful, informed, and well thought out decision. For Madison's part, it was lifesaving, as six year old dogs are not at the top of the desirability list of most potential adopters.

"She is definitely overweight and could use a good exercise routine to help her health," said the shelter staffer to Madison's new guardians.

"Hmmm…" they replied, "so could we."

Surma

Even after long, difficult days of dealing with the homeless animal problem on the job, many shelter workers take it home with them at night, too. Literally.

Surma and her sister arrived at the shelter as strays. The staffer who took them in noted in their records, "These little babies are pretty young – four to five weeks – but are very social. They are eating well (however messily) and seem strong." Still, they were undersized and several weeks shy of being ready for adoption. The notes continued, "I washed them off and flea combed them. They are very sweet. I think they would do okay in an experienced foster home."

It is not uncommon for staffers who care for animals at the shelter to also open their homes to them. Indeed, when faced with animals who have needs that the shelter cannot meet, it can seem like the *only* thing to do.

A staff person offered to provide a foster home to Surma and her sister so they could have time to get a little bigger and a little older. They lived with him and received his skilled care for nearly four weeks, and when they were ready, he brought them back to the shelter to go up for adoption. He gave them the Indian names Surma and Kajol, and posted hand-written cards on their cage, describing their personalities and revealing his affection for them: "Kajol is a cuddler. She seeks out companions for play, lap sits, and purring. She loves to explore. Surma is playful and independent. She is very inquisitive and very affectionate."

In a exceptional stroke of good fortune, an adopter came to the shelter who wanted to adopt two kittens. It is rare for littermates to be adopted to the same home – most adopters want, or are prepared for, just one animal. It must be bewildering for those left behind as each of their siblings are adopted and inexplicably, to them, gone, after spending every moment since birth in each other's company. But these sisters would be growing up, and growing old, together.

The staffer who fostered the kittens handled their adoption, and when the paperwork was completed, the new collars and tags put on the kittens, and the cat carriers assembled, he asked quietly, "Can I say goodbye to them?"

He whispered softly in their kitten ears things the rest of us could not hear. Perhaps he said he'd miss them. Perhaps he told them to be good girls. Perhaps he told them what the rest of us were thinking, and wishing, and hoping: *Good luck... be safe... have a long, happy life.*

ANOTHER WEEK BEGINS

One week in an American animal shelter quickly, but unforgettably, passes. By our seventh day, we had met hundreds of animals. We'd photographed many of them, read their records, petted them and played with them. We watched some begin new lives and watched others die. We documented their stories and watched their fates unfold.

We felt attached to them, protective of them. They were "our" animals, the ones we knew, the ones whose stories we would tell.

Our week in the shelter concluded, we would now turn to the writing. We were gathering our things and getting ready to leave when the next lost dog was brought into the shelter. And then a feral cat.

Another dog was brought back from a foster home to go up for adoption. A mother cat gave birth in her cage to a litter of kittens. A dog was surrendered by his guardian, and then another lost dog was brought in.

A new week begins. And across the country, in shelters just like this one, animals just like "ours" are arriving, by the hundreds. Then thousands. Then millions. One at a time.

name unknown

Brought in stray. Red collar; injured foot.

no name

Brought in stray. Feral.

Jenny

Returned from foster home to go up for adoption.

name unknown

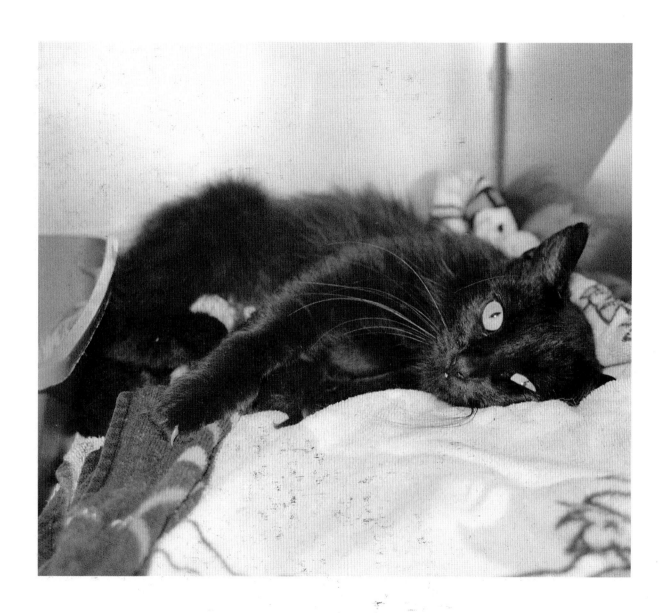

Brought in stray. Gave birth to three kittens.

Tyson

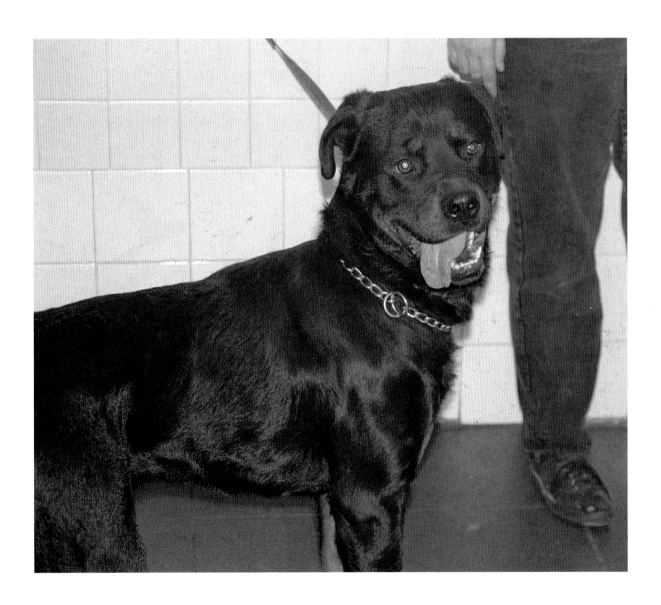

REASON FOR SURRENDER: "Landlord doesn't approve."

Kendall

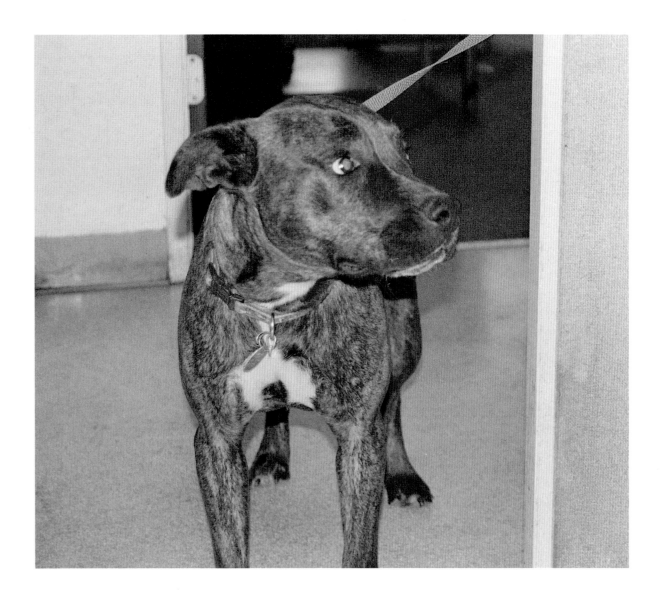

Brought in stray. Chasing livestock; third time in shelter.

AFTERWORD

We are aware that this book has been a hard read. It was, as you can imagine, difficult to write. We had many grief-filled days and sleepless nights. We raged and we cried. The animals in this book entered our hearts, became part of us, and they have been with us as we moved through every part of our writing.

"Before we can fix our troubled relationship with nature, we must be willing to look at it."

— Derrick Jensen

If you have come this far, read these chapters and are still here, we thank you – it is nothing less than an act of courage to look past the statistics and to allow yourself to see the individuals, to look into their eyes and read about their lives, to bear witness to their stories. Probably many people who picked this book up did not finish it, so difficult is the reality it shows. But it is, on all levels, the truth, and we believe that truth must be told, difficult though it may be.

You may be angered by reading this book. As you should be – it is right to be angry. But not at the book itself. Be angry at the truth the book tells.

You may have found it painful to read this book. As we all should – it is right to feel hurt. Remember that our pain tells us we have caring hearts and deep compassion, and that those things are still alive and well within us.

We can be angry, and we can be hurt, but we must not turn away.

Before we can change something, we must be willing to look at it. With this book we have taken that first step.

A friend asks us, where is the *hope* in this sad situation? Is there hope in animal shelters, in those kennels and cages? She asks, is there hope in your book?

We believe we know the answer to her questions: the hope is *you*, reader, in the very fact that these stories – these animals – moved you, even broke your heart. The hope is in your anger and your hurt, and in what these animals taught you, and what you do with those lessons.

We offer this book in honor of the animals in it, as testament to what they went through. We offer it so their lives will not be in vain, so they will not be invisible, and so their stories may teach us all. We offer this book in *hope*.

How do we end this tragedy? What can we do? The answers are multi-faceted, but they're not difficult. As the animals in this book have shown us, the most basic answers to the homeless animal problem are in our everyday actions: always keeping current

"The hope for the animals of tomorrow is to be found in a human culture which learns to feel beyond itself. We must learn empathy, we must learn to see into the eyes of an animal and feel that its life has value because it is alive. Nothing less will do."

— Kenneth White

ID on our animals and ensuring they are kept safe and do not become lost. Spaying and neutering to help end overpopulation. Getting an animal only when we're absolutely ready, and then learning and taking the time to select the right companion to make a good match that will work, for the animal and for us. Saving a life in jeopardy by adopting a homeless animal from a shelter or rescue group. And making an unconditional, unwavering commitment to that animal for his entire lifetime.

These basic, yet powerful solutions are in our hands. Shelters should be leaders in the battle to end the homeless animal tragedy, but they cannot end it for us. Shelters should, and must, create programs that reach out beyond their walls to prevent animals from becoming homeless – identification and microchipping programs, low cost spay/neuter, pet parenting classes and animal behavior help, for instance – but we must use these programs. We are the ones who must make the commitment, and take the actions, to ensure we never cause an animal to be in an animal shelter. We must understand: as soon as this country stops filling animal shelters with homeless animals, the killing can stop.

Ultimately, though, we need to transcend sheltering and the current shelter system in this country. The shelter system, as it exists today, and has existed for decades, has as one of its primary functions the processing of living beings – either by recycling them to new homes or destroying them, but disposing of them somehow and relieving people and communities of their responsibility for them. It is a tangible sign of our society's deep disconnection from other beings, a disconnection so profound and damaging that we could legitimately categorize it as a sickness.

We need to acknowledge this sickness and how it plays out in our shelters, and never make excuses for it or believe that it is acceptable. The truth is, there should not be a need in a civilized society for a system that disposes of animals as if they were trash. We need to tell this truth, as an act of respect to the animals, and because the truth cannot be changed until it can be seen.

At the deepest level, the only thing that will heal this sickness, and alleviate the pain we feel over this issue, is to end the killing, by creating communities that no longer have overwhelming homeless animal problems and have, therefore, no need to kill animals. By creating communities that find killing to be an unacceptable answer, and that see animals as having value and beauty,

as beings with a sacred spark of life and spirit.

People sometimes ask, in light of the devastating and important issues that face us in our modern times, why the homeless animal issue is important, why we should be concerned about it. The answer to this question is critical, as the underlying societal values that enable the homeless animal problem also enable and are deeply connected to other social issues of our time – issues which exist on a continuum created by our attitudes toward our fellow beings and the planet we share.

The homeless animal problem is a reflection of a society that has lost touch with other living beings, with the natural world, and with the very web of life. It is but one tragic symptom of a culture that does not see its connections to others, does not see others as having inherent value, and instead sees them as put here for our use, as disposable or somehow lesser, as somehow not worthy of reverence, compassion and respect. This same societal thinking, this way of separating ourselves from "others," allows for the possibility of the destruction of ancient forests, damage to our environment and the animals in it, of racism and exploitation of third world peoples, of poverty and human homelessness, of children going hungry in a land of plenty, of devaluing our elders... this way of viewing the "others" in our world enables and underlies a continuum of issues.

> "We owe it to ourselves and the animal world as well to create, not merely a body of rules and regulations to govern our conduct, but a level of sensibility that makes us care, deeply and constructively, about the entire planet and all of its varied inhabitants. If we can accomplish this, then perhaps, some far-off day, those who follow us down the track of the generations will be able to dwell in relative harmony with all of the creatures of the earth, human and non-human."
>
> — William Kunstler

The systematic mass destruction and disposal of millions of living creatures every year constitutes a kind of violence in our society that is no less violent because it is institutionalized and mostly overlooked. When killing those who are closest to, and most dependent upon us becomes an unquestioned fact of daily life, we have set a very dangerous and damaging precedent as to what is ethically acceptable, what we are willing to tolerate, and what we are capable of doing to others. How much easier is it to deny consideration and compassion to one group when we have learned to accept the mass killing of another – and especially, of beings whom we call our "friends"?

The homeless animal issue is critically important because it is so fundamental: dogs and cats are the closest most people ever get to other species and the natural world. If our concern and compassion are so weak and limited that we are unable to save those animals closest to us, how will we ever be able to save the more distant beings – the endangered species we may never see, the redwoods and mountains and wilderness we may never visit, the suffering people we may never meet and whose misery we may never experience directly?

And yet, there is unique power in this issue. Solving this problem offers us the chance to take a first step toward healing our relationship with the natural world, to reawaken and embrace our connection with other living beings, to reaffirm the preciousness of life itself. It offers us the potent opportunity to become better human beings, to call forward the finest parts of ourselves and express the very best of our humanity. If we are able, as a society, to find the compassion and dedication to save our companion animals, to treat them with the love and respect they deserve, to solve this problem in an ethical way, then perhaps we can extend that compassion and dedication to others in need.

Perhaps this issue can be a stepping stone toward an expanding circle of compassion and action, toward creating a society that is just and caring to all living beings – beginning with the precious ones "right in our own backyards."

The two cats who live with me, Otto and Raphael, walk into the room as I write. They swirl around my feet, nibble at some food, look out the window. One huge black cat, one skinny orange one, each with his own unique, quirky personality, each with his own story.

They are ordinary cats: six years old now, they have lived in my home since their kittenhoods, and are healthy, safe, and happy. They play and pick on each other, follow the sun each day from window to window, sleep in deep peace.

And they are extraordinary cats: they shine into my life their unconditional love, share with me their in-the-moment wisdom, show me how to live with generosity, gentleness, and joy. Their innocent presence is a constant reminder of the preciousness of all life.

> "Kindness and compassion toward all living things is the mark of a civilized society.... Racism, economic deprival, dog fighting and cock fighting, bullfighting and rodeos are cut from the same fabric: violence."
>
> — César Chávez

> "We need another and a wiser and a perhaps more mystical concept of animals.... We patronize them for their incompleteness, for their tragic fate of having taken form so far below ourselves. And therein we err and err greatly. For the animal shall not be measured by man. In a world older and more complete than ours, they move finished and complete, gifted with extensions of the senses we have lost or never attained, living by voices we shall never hear. They are not brethren; they are not underlings; they are other nations, caught with ourselves in the net of life and time, fellow prisoners of the splendor and travail of the earth."
>
> — Henry Beston

Our companion animals live with us in our world, but they bring with them gifts from their animal worlds. It is a privilege to have them near. They are our link to the wild animals we will never see except in books or on television. They are the animal fur we get to stroke, and the paws we get to touch. They are the wild, mysterious eyes we get to gaze into. They give us a glimpse into "other nations." They are messengers, bringing us a critical, sacred message of connection; they are teachers, showing us back to our place in the web of life, showing us the way back home.

Can there be any doubt of what we owe them in return?

Honoring Them All

During the week this book was written...
363 animals passed through the shelter:

249 were brought in lost or stray
97 were surrendered by their guardians
14 were brought in for euthanasia due to illness or old age
3 were taken in under protective custody

15 were found and claimed by their families
6 were dead on arrival
6 died after arriving
2 were stolen
2 were transferred to other shelters
215 were adopted to new homes
117 were euthanized

Remembering and paying tribute to each of them...

A065588, A FEMALE BLACK CAT, ADOPTED ❤ A065592, POKEMON, A MALE BLACK KITTEN MISSING ONE EYE, BREED RESCUED ❤ A066378, MISS PRISS, A FEMALE BLACK CAT, ADOPTED ❤ A066379, A FEMALE BLACK CAT, EUTHANIZED ❤ A065593, RUBY, A NEUTERED MALE BLACK CAT, ADOPTED ❤ A066541, A NEUTERED ORANGE TABBY CAT, OLDER, WITH A WEAK HIND END, ADOPTED ❤ A065201, FRANKLIN, A MALE GRAY AND WHITE KITTEN, ADOPTED ❤ A064462, PEARL, A SPAYED FEMALE PASTEL TORTOISE SHELL CAT, EUTHANIZED ❤ A063674, A NEUTERED MALE BLACK CAT, STOLEN ❤ A063662, INGRID, A FEMALE TORTOISE SHELL CAT, ADOPTED ❤ A065127, MAX, A MALE SEAL POINT CAT, ADOPTED ❤ A066322, NAUGHTY, A FEMALE ORANGE TIGER CAT, BREED RESCUED ❤ A066617, A MALE WHITE KITTEN, ADOPTED ❤ A064793, CHRISTMAN, A MALE BLACK KITTEN, ADOPTED ❤ A064243, KATIE, A FEMALE TORTOISE SHELL CAT, EUTHANIZED ❤ A066581, ZOEY, A FEMALE BLACK KITTEN, EUTHANIZED ❤ A066624, A MALE GRAY TIGER CAT, EUTHANIZED ❤ A066191, A MALE BLACK KITTEN, EUTHANIZED ❤ A066709, ISIS, A FEMALE BLACK CAT, TRANSFERRED TO ANOTHER SHELTER ❤ A066710, MINI T, A MALE BLACK KITTEN, ADOPTED ❤ A066897, SEX UNKNOWN, A BLACK KITTEN, EUTHANIZED ❤ A067697, MISTER GREEN, A MALE BLACK KITTEN, ADOPTED ❤ A066896, MISSY, A FEMALE BLACK KITTEN, ADOPTED ❤ A067695, THE GIRL, A FEMALE BLACK KITTEN, ADOPTED ❤ A067830, MISTER YELLOW, A MALE BLACK KITTEN, ADOPTED ❤ A067696, LITTLE BLUE, A MALE BLACK KITTEN, ADOPTED ❤ A066706, MAI TAI, A MALE SEAL POINT KITTEN, ADOPTED ❤ A066707, PANTERA, A MALE BLACK KITTEN, ADOPTED ❤ A066708, A MALE BLACK KITTEN, ADOPTED ❤ A066430, A MALE BLACK AND WHITE KITTEN, ADOPTED ❤ A064835, SIRINA, A FEMALE BLACK YOUNG ADULT CAT WITH FIVE KITTENS, ADOPTED ❤ A066439, A MALE BLACK CAT, EUTHANIZED ❤ A066370, CARLY, A FEMALE BUFF TIGER KITTEN, ADOPTED ❤ A065679, A FEMALE BROWN TIGER CAT WITH WHITE ON CHEST AND PAWS, ADOPTED ❤ A066638, A NEUTERED MALE BLACK AND WHITE CAT WITH A NOTCHED LEFT EAR, EUTHANIZED ❤ A066667, A FEMALE TABBY/CALICO KITTEN, EUTHANIZED ❤ A066287, A FEMALE GRAY CAT WEARING A BLUE FLEA COLLAR, EUTHANIZED ❤ A066677, MANXIE, A FEMALE BLACK PREGNANT CAT, EUTHANIZED ❤ A066352, SADIE, A SPAYED FEMALE CALICO CAT, ADOPTED ❤A066606, A FEMALE BROWN AND WHITE KITTEN, ADOPTED ❤ A066652, A FEMALE BLACK KITTEN, ADOPTED ❤ A066653, A FEMALE BLACK AND WHITE KITTEN, ADOPTED ❤ A066654, A FEMALE AGOUTI KITTEN, EUTHANIZED ❤ A066655, A FEMALE AGOUTI KITTEN, ADOPTED ❤ A066686,

BONKERS, A NEUTERED MALE BLACK CAT, EUTHANIZED ❤ A066057, FRISKY, A SPAYED FEMALE CALICO CAT, ADOPTED ❤ A066575, BIGFOOT, A NEUTERED MALE ORANGE TIGER WITH BLACK ON NOSE AND FACE, ADOPTED ❤ A066696, FORREST, A MALE FLAME POINT KITTEN ADOPTED ❤ A066490, ROGER, A NEUTERED MALE BLACK AND WHITE CAT, ADOPTED ❤ A066386, A FEMALE BLACK KITTEN, ADOPTED ❤ A066623, EBONY, A SPAYED FEMALE BLACK CAT, EUTHANIZED ❤ A066388, A MALE ORANGE TIGER CAT, EUTHANIZED ❤ A064203, PABLO, A NEUTERED MALE BROWN TABBY CAT, ADOPTED ❤ A064544, LACY, A FEMALE BROWN TABBY KITTEN, ADOPTED ❤ A064739, MAX, A MALE BLACK KITTEN, EUTHANIZED ❤ A065776, JAKE, A MALE BLACK KITTEN, ADOPTED ❤ A066515, A MALE WHITE AND GRAY KITTEN WITH SIAMESE MARKINGS, STOLEN ❤ A066565, HAPPY, A FEMALE BROWN, BLACK AND GRAY TABBY CAT, ADOPTED ❤ A066657, AMBER, A SPAYED FEMALE TORTOISE SHELL POINT CAT WEARING A BLUE CANVAS COLLAR WITH A BELL, ADOPTED ❤ A063661, BLONDIE, A MALE WHITE AND CREAM KITTEN, ADOPTED ❤ A065175, OSCAR, A NEUTERED MALE BROWN TIGER CAT, ADOPTED ❤ A065395, MINNIE, A SPAYED FEMALE WHITE KITTEN WITH BLACK SPOTS ON HER HEAD, BACK AND TAIL, ADOPTED ❤ A066046, LILLY, A FEMALE BLACK CAT, EUTHANIZED ❤ A066582, A NEUTERED MALE BROWN TIGER CAT, EUTHANIZED ❤ A066651, A FEMALE BROWN TIGER KITTEN, ADOPTED ❤ A066219, FRANKLIN, A MALE BLACK AND WHITE CAT, ADOPTED ❤ A066672, JASMINE, A FEMALE BROWN TORTOISE SHELL POINT CAT, ADOPTED ❤ A066674, PINKY, A MALE WHITE FLAME POINT KITTEN, ADOPTED ❤ A066687, COLE, A MALE BLACK AND WHITE KITTEN, ADOPTED ❤ A066688, MADONNA, A FEMALE BROWN TIGER KITTEN, ADOPTED ❤ A065539, LITTLE MAMA, A FEMALE BLACK CAT, EUTHANIZED ❤ A066658, A FEMALE BROWN TABBY CAT WITH ORANGE PATCHES, EUTHANIZED ❤ A066681, ALIE, A FEMALE GRAY CAT, ADOPTED ❤ A066682, A LITTER OF FIVE GRAY KITTENS, ALL BREED RESCUED ❤ A066607, A MALE BLACK CAT WITH WHITE ON HIS CHEST, EUTHANIZED ❤ A065202, JAKE, A MALE BLACK KITTEN WITH WHITE ON HIS CHEST AND BACK, ADOPTED ❤ A065203, SPLAT, A FEMALE BLACK AND WHITE KITTEN WITH BLACK DOTS ON HER WHITE FACE, ADOPTED ❤ A065728, ANNABELL, A FEMALE BLACK AND WHITE CAT, ADOPTED ❤ A065518, A FEMALE TORTOISE SHELL CAT WITH A TAN FACE, ADOPTED ❤ A066280, BABY, A NEUTERED MALE WHITE AND BLACK CAT WITH A BLACK STRIPE ON HIS HEAD, ADOPTED ❤ A064290, WHEAT THIN, A MALE BLACK KITTEN, ADOPTED ❤ A064317, TRISCUIT, A MALE BLACK KITTEN, ADOPTED ❤ A065869, THEODORE, A NEUTERED MALE BROWN TIGER CAT, ADOPTED ❤ A066071, SALLY, A FEMALE BLACK CAT, EUTHANIZED ❤ A066076, BUDDY, A MALE BLACK CAT, EUTHANIZED ❤ A066536, A FEMALE GRAY CAT WITH A WHITE SPOT ON HER NECK, ADOPTED ❤ A066627, A LITTER OF FIVE BLACK KITTENS, EUTHANIZED ❤ A066305, PETER PAN, A NEUTERED MALE BLACK TIGER CAT WITH A WHITE NOSE, FEET AND CHEST, ADOPTED ❤ A066284, A NEUTERED MALE GRAY TIGER CAT, ADOPTED ❤ A065885, CAMI, A SPAYED FEMALE BLACK AND WHITE CAT, ADOPTED ❤ A066179, SASSY, A FEMALE CALICO KITTEN, ADOPTED ❤ A066325, A MALE BLACK SMOKE CAT, EUTHANIZED ❤ A065900, A NEUTERED MALE BLACK CAT, EUTHANIZED ❤ A066403, A NEUTERED MALE ORANGE TABBY CAT OVER WHITE, EUTHANIZED ❤ A065125, SNORKLER, A MALE GRAY TIGER KITTEN, ADOPTED ❤ A065464, SMOKEY, A MALE BLACK KITTEN WITH A WHITE SPOT ON HIS CHEST, EUTHANIZED ❤ A065451, JOEY, A MALE BLACK TABBY CAT, ADOPTED ❤ A065124, SPIKE, A MALE GRAY TABBY CAT WITH WHITE, ADOPTED ❤ A064895, BABY TIGGER, A MALE GRAY TIGER KITTEN, ADOPTED ❤ A064445, HERCULES, MALE BLACK KITTEN, ADOPTED ❤ A065200, BAKER, A MALE GRAY AND WHITE KITTEN, ADOPTED ❤ A065236, TINY, A FEMALE BROWN TIGER CAT OVER WHITE, ADOPTED ❤ A065350, SCRUNCHIE, A MALE ORANGE TIGER KITTEN WITH WHITE ON HIS FACE, ADOPTED ❤ A065424, A MALE BLACK AND WHITE KITTEN, EUTHANIZED ❤ A065681, BISCUIT, A MALE GRAY AND WHITE KITTEN, ADOPTED ❤ A065745, MOMMO, A SPAYED FEMALE GRAY CAT, ADOPTED ❤ A065856, POTATO SALAD, A MALE ORANGE TIGER KITTEN, EUTHANIZED ❤ A065857, COLESLAW, A FEMALE GRAY TIGER KITTEN, ADOPTED ❤ A065977, KAJOL, A FEMALE WHITE KITTEN WITH BLACK PATCHES, ADOPTED ❤ A065978, SURMA, A FEMALE TORTOISE SHELL KITTEN WITH SOME WHITE MARKINGS, ADOPTED ❤ A067503, A MALE BLACK AND WHITE KITTEN, ADOPTED ❤ A067504, FLUFFY, A FEMALE GRAY TIGER KITTEN, ADOPTED ❤ A067698, IGGY, A MALE BLACK KITTEN, ADOPTED ❤ A067502, HARRY, A MALE GRAY KITTEN, ADOPTED ❤ A067501, GRAY KITTEN, SEX UNKNOWN, DIED AT FOSTER HOME ❤ A067832, MALE BLACK CAT, BREED RESCUED ❤ A067700, BETH, A FEMALE GRAY TABBY KITTEN, ADOPTED ❤ A067699, GEORGE, A MALE BROWN TABBY KITTEN, ADOPTED ❤ A066080, A SPAYED FEMALE GREY TABBY CAT, BREED RESCUED ❤ A066190, A MALE BLACK AND WHITE KITTEN, ADOPTED ❤ A067040, A MALE BLACK AND WHITE KITTEN, ADOPTED ❤ A067042, A MALE BLACK AND WHITE KITTEN, ADOPTED ❤ A066198, SABLE, A SPAYED FEMALE SEAL POINT SIAMESE CAT, ADOPTED ❤ A066199, PRIMROSE, A FEMALE BLACK TIGER KITTEN OVER WHITE, ADOPTED ❤ A067964, SPRITE, A SPAYED FEMALE BLACK AND WHITE CAT, ADOPTED ❤ A067960, WINNIE, A FEMALE BROWN TIGER KITTEN, ADOPTED ❤ A067643, EARL, A NEUTERED MALE BLACK AND WHITE CAT,

BREED RESCUED ❤ A066222, A FEMALE WHITE CALICO KITTEN, ADOPTED ❤ A066223, A FEMALE CALICO KITTEN, ADOPTED ❤ A066226, A MALE TIGER KITTEN BLACK OVER WHITE, EUTHANIZED ❤ A066227, A MALE BUFF TIGER KITTEN, ADOPTED ❤ A066721, BUFFY, A MALE BUFF TIGER, ADOPTED ❤ A066258, A MALE GRAY KITTEN WITH WHITE PAWS, ADOPTED ❤ A066847, A FEMALE PASTEL TORTOISE SHELL KITTEN, ADOPTED ❤ A066845, A FEMALE PASTEL TORTOISE SHELL KITTEN, ADOPTED ❤ A066846, A MALE GRAY TIGER KITTEN, ADOPTED ❤ A066260, A FEMALE ORANGE TABBY KITTEN OVER WHITE, ADOPTED ❤ A066331, A FEMALE BUFF TIGER KITTEN, BREED RESCUED ❤ A066389, MINKY, A SPAYED FEMALE BROWN TIGER CAT, ADOPTED ❤ A066390, A FEMALE PASTEL TORTOISE SHELL KITTEN, ADOPTED ❤ A066399, SMOKEY, A FEMALE TORTOISE SHELL KITTEN, ADOPTED ❤ A066679, A BROWN TIGER CAT, SEX UNKNOWN, EUTHANIZED ❤ A066680, A BLACK CAT, SEX UNKNOWN, EUTHANIZED ❤ A066718, AN ORANGE CAT, SEX UNKNOWN, DIED AT VETERINARIAN ❤ A065935, PANCHA, A FEMALE BLACK RETRIEVER MIX, ADOPTED ❤ A066351, MISHA, A BLACK AND BROWN ROTTWEILER/PIT BULL PUPPY MIX, EUTHANIZED ❤ A066300, MAX, A MALE BLACK AND TAN SHEPHERD MIX, ADOPTED ❤ A066530, CALVIN, A NEUTERED MALE BUFF SPANIEL/ GOLDEN RETRIEVER MIX, ADOPTED ❤ A066493, A NEUTERED MALE BLUE MERLE AUSTRALIAN CATTLE DOG MIX WEARING A BLUE NYLON COLLAR, EUTHANIZED ❤ A066480, A MALE CREME AND WHITE AKITA MIX WEARING A BLACK COLLAR, EUTHANIZED ❤ A066656, KELLI, A FEMALE WHITE AND BUFF TERRIER MIX, EUTHANIZED ❤ A066713, ATHENA, A SPAYED FEMALE BLACK LABRADOR RETRIEVER MIX WITH MANGE AROUND HER EYES, RECLAIMED ❤ A066443, WALLY, A NEUTERED MALE BLACK LABRADOR RETRIEVER MIX WITH A PURPLE TONGUE, ADOPTED ❤ A066692, MADISON, A FEMALE BROWN SHEPHERD MIX, ADOPTED ❤ A066685, CHUTNEY, A MALE BLACK LABRADOR RETRIEVER MIX, EUTHANIZED ❤ A065735, RYJA, A NEUTERED MALE BLACK CHOW MIX WEARING A BLACK NYLON COLLAR, ADOPTED ❤ A065330, A MALE BLACK AUSTRALIAN CATTLE DOG, ADOPTED ❤ A066615, JOEY, A MALE BLACK GERMAN SHEPHERD MIX, ADOPTED ❤ A066675, A NEUTERED MALE BROWN STANDARD POODLE WEARING A GREEN NYLON COLLAR, ADOPTED ❤ A065297, BUBBA TWO, A NEUTERED MALE BLACK DOBERMAN WEARING A CHOKE CHAIN, ADOPTED ❤ A066630, SPORT, A MALE TAN RHODESIAN RIDGEBACK MIX, EUTHANIZED ❤ A066700, HUGH, A MALE BRINDLE BULL MASTIFF WEARING A BLUE NYLON COLLAR, RECLAIMED ❤ A066701, SIGMUND, A MALE BRINDLE BULL MASTIFF WEARING A GREEN NYLON COLLAR, RECLAIMED ❤ A066126, SADI, A SPAYED WHITE SHEPHERD MIX WEARING A TAN NYLON COLLAR, ADOPTED ❤ A066145, BUCK, A NEUTERED MALE BLACK AND BROWN DOBERMAN MIX, WEARING A SILVER CHOKE CHAIN, EUTHANIZED ❤ A066539, LYKOS, A MALE BLACK AND BROWN GERMAN SHEPHERD MIX, WEARING A BLACK NYLON COLLAR, ADOPTED ❤ A066487, A FEMALE TRICOLOR AUSTRALIAN SHEPHERD MIX, EUTHANIZED ❤ A066432, ALICE, A FEMALE BLACK AND BUFF SHEPHERD MIX, EUTHANIZED ❤ A006572, BEETHOVEN, A NEUTERED MALE BLACK AND BUFF GERMAN SHEPHERD MIX, WEARING A BROWN LEATHER COLLAR, EUTHANIZED ❤ A066212, PRETTY BOY, A NEUTERED MALE BLACK AND CREAM GERMAN SHEPHERD MIX, ADOPTED ❤A065695, BOGIE, A MALE BROWN AND BLACK AMERICAN PIT BULL, WEARING A BROWN LEATHER COLLAR, ADOPTED ❤ A050209, JAKE, A NEUTERED MALE BUFF GOLDEN RETRIEVER/CHOW, WEARING A BROWN LEATHER COLLAR, ADOPTED ❤ A066637, CARLIE, A SPAYED FEMALE BLACK LABRADOR RETRIEVER MIX, ADOPTED ❤ A065554, PORKCHOP, A MALE BROWN MERLE AND WHITE AMERICAN BULLDOG WEARING A RED NYLON COLLAR, ADOPTED ❤ A066592, A MALE TAN AND WHITE PIT BULL MIX, WEARING A BLACK NYLON COLLAR, EUTHANIZED ❤ A066215, MOLLY, A FEMALE WHITE AMERICAN PIT BULL TERRIER WITH BROWN SPOTS ON EARS, EUTHANIZED ❤ A066382, MARVIN, A MALE BLACK LABRADOR RETRIEVER, EUTHANIZED ❤ A066065, RUBY, A FEMALE BLACK AMERICAN PIT BULL TERRIER MIX WITH WHITE ON HER NOSE, NECK AND TIP OF TAIL, EUTHANIZED ❤ A066241, SANDY, A NEUTERED MALE BUFF GOLDEN RETRIEVER MIX WEARING A RED NYLON COLLAR, ADOPTED ❤ A066013, LADY, A FEMALE TRI-COLOR BLUE TICK COON HOUND, ADOPTED ❤ A066014, DUKE, A MALE TRI-COLOR BLUE TICK COON HOUND, ADOPTED ❤ A066691, SASHA, A SPAYED FEMALE BLACK LABRADOR RETRIEVER, ADOPTED ❤ A066631, A MALE BLACK ROTTWEILER WEARING A RED CANVAS COLLAR, EUTHANIZED ❤ A019494, APOLLO, A MALE HARLEQUIN GREAT DANE WEARING A BROWN COLLAR, DIED ❤ A066636, A NEUTERED MALE BLACK ROTTWEILER, EUTHANIZED ❤ A066702, CHINO, A NEUTERED MALE CHOCOLATE LABRADOR RETRIEVER MIX WEARING A BLACK PLASTIC COLLAR, ADOPTED ❤ A065149, THOR, A MALE BLACK ROTTWEILER WEARING A SILVER CHOKE CHAIN, RECLAIMED ❤ A062967, NIPPER, A NEUTERED MALE BLACK AND BROWN ROTTWEILER MIX, EUTHANIZED ❤ A038561, BETTY, A SPAYED FEMALE BLACK AND TAN AUSTRALIAN CATTLE DOG, RECLAIMED ❤ A063384, GATOR, A NEUTERED MALE BLACK AND TAN ROTTWEILER MIX, EUTHANIZED ❤ A062943, JENNY, A FEMALE BLACK AND TAN ROTTWEILER MIX, EUTHANIZED ❤ A065954, CHARLIE, A NEUTERED MALE BLACK AND TAN DOBERMAN MIX, EUTHANIZED ❤ A066214, BARKLEY, A MALE GRAY TERRIER MIX WITH WHITE ON HIS CHEST AND LEGS, ADOPTED ❤A066120, CHANDI,

A FEMALE GRAY AND WHITE AMERICAN PIT BULL TERRIER MIX, ADOPTED ❤ A066570, RELF, A NEUTERED MALE GOLDEN RETRIEVER MIX WITH WHITE ON HIS CHEST AND STOMACH AND WEARING A BROWN LEATHER COLLAR, ADOPTED ❤ A066574, SIMBA, A MALE BLACK AND TAN CHOW MIX, ADOPTED ❤ A066573, SHE-DEVIL, A FEMALE TAN AND BLACK RHODESIAN RIDGEBACK PUPPY MIX, BREED RESCUED ❤ A064725, SGT. LEE, A MALE TAN CHINESE SHARPEI, DIED AT VETERINARIAN'S ❤ A066678, VINCENT VAN GOAT, A NEUTERED MALE BROWN AND BLACK GOAT WITH MUTILATED EARS, BREED RESCUED ❤ A065704, A MALE WHITE CHICKEN, EUTHANIZED ❤ A065706, A MALE WHITE CHICKEN, EUTHANIZED ❤ A065707, A MALE WHITE CHICKEN, ADOPTED ❤ A065708, A MALE WHITE CHICKEN, ADOPTED ❤ A065709, A MALE WHITE CHICKEN, ADOPTED ❤ A066384, A MALE RED CHICKEN, ADOPTED ❤ A066385, A MALE RED CHICKEN, ADOPTED ❤ A066424, A FEMALE BLACK CALIFORNIAN RABBIT, ADOPTED ❤ A062930, MUFFY, A FEMALE WHITE NEW ZEALAND RABBIT, EUTHANIZED ❤ A062931, FLUFFY, A FEMALE WHITE NEW ZEALAND RABBIT, EUTHANIZED ❤ A065871, PRINCE CHARLES, A MALE WHITE HIMALAYAN RABBIT, EUTHANIZED ❤ A066504, A FEMALE GRAY CALIFORNIAN RABBIT WITH BROWN EARS AND BROWN FEET, BREED RESCUED ❤ A066088, A FEMALE RED CHICKEN, ADOPTED ❤ A063539, A MALE BLACK RABBIT, EUTHANIZED ❤ A063857, A FEMALE BROWN RABBIT WITH WHITE BACK LEGS AND BELLY, BREED RESCUED ❤ A064398, A FEMALE WHITE RABBIT WITH BROWN NOSE, EARS AND FEET, BREED RESCUED ❤ A063538, A MALE BLACK RABBIT, EUTHANIZED ❤ A065951, ELLIOT, A MALE TRICOLOR BANTAM CHICKEN, ADOPTED ❤ A066339, A MALE WHITE MOUSE, DIED ❤ A066586, A LITTER OF 3 RED-EARED SLIDER TURTLES, ADOPTED ❤ A065829, CLEVER, A MALE WHITE MOUSE ADOPTED ❤ A066060, CANELA, A FEMALE WHITE AND GRAY HAMSTER, ADOPTED ❤ A066062, FOUR FEMALE BROWN HAMSTERS ADOPTED ❤ A066537, HERCULES, A MALE TRICOLOR GUINEA PIG, ADOPTED ❤ A066578, A FEMALE BLACK RAT WITH A LARGE TUMOR ON HER ABDOMEN, BREED RESCUED ❤ A066579, A FEMALE GRAY RAT, BREED RESCUED ❤ A066720, KARL, A MALE BEAGLE WEARING A BLACK LEATHER COLLAR, RECLAIMED ❤ A066723, HANNAH, A FEMALE BLACK LABRADOR RETRIEVER WEARING A RED CANVAS COLLAR, RECLAIMED ❤ A066725, BREE, FEMALE BLACK AND WHITE AUSTRALIAN CATTLE DOG, ADOPTED ❤ A063792, KHAKY, A SPAYED FEMALE BROWN AMERICAN PIT BULL TERRIER MIX, RECLAIMED ❤ A066718, AN ORANGE CAT, SEX UNKNOWN, DEAD ON ARRIVAL ❤ A066727, ENRI, A NEUTERED MALE GREY TABBY CAT, EUTHANIZED AT GUARDIAN'S REQUEST ❤ A066734, CISCO, A MALE BRINDLE SHEPHERD MIX, EUTHANIZED AT GUARDIAN'S REQUEST ❤ A065331, DOLLY, A SPAYED FEMALE BUFF TABBY CAT, EUTHANIZED AT GUARDIAN'S REQUEST ❤ A066738, POOH, A SPAYED FEMALE ORANGE CAT, EUTHANIZED AT GUARDIAN'S REQUEST ❤ A066746, A MALE AUSTRALIAN CATTLE DOG/ROTTWEILER MIX WEARING A SILVER CHOKE CHAIN, EUTHANIZED ❤ A066726, A BUFF TIGER CAT, SEX UNKOWN, EUTHANIZED ❤ A066757, OZZY, A NEUTERED MALE TAN AND WHITE CORGI/CHIHUAHUA MIX, ADOPTED ❤ A066758, BELLA, A FEMALE BLACK AND TAN ROTTWEILER MIX, ADOPTED ❤ A066759, CLEOPATRA, A FEMALE SILVER AND BLACK KEESHUND WEARING A MULTI-COLORED COLLAR, RECLAIMED ❤ A066729, A NEUTERED MALE BROWN TIGER CAT, ADOPTED ❤ A066731, A MALE BLACK CAT, EUTHANIZED ❤ A066744, A NEUTERED MALE BLACK CAT, EUTHANIZED ❤ A066748, A FEMALE WHITE SEAL POINT CAT, EUTHANIZED ❤ A066725, A WHITE CAT, SEX UNKNOWN, DEAD ON ARRIVAL ❤ A066732, GUINEVIERE, A FEMALE GRAY TIGER KITTEN, ADOPTED ❤ A066752, LANCELOT, A MALE GRAY TABBY KITTEN, ADOPTED ❤ A066754, A FEMALE WHITE HOTOT RABBIT WITH DARK GRAY SPOTS, BREED RESCUED ❤ A066544, A MALE WHITE RABBIT, BREED RESCUED ❤ A063994, GABE, A MALE TAN AND BLACK GERMAN SHEPHERD MIX, EUTHANIZED ❤ A066736, SOX, A NEUTERED MALE BLACK SMOKE CAT WITH TUXEDO MARKINGS, ADOPTED ❤ A066735, CAMILLE, A FEMALE TORTOISE SHELL CAT, EUTHANIZED ❤ A066750, A FEMALE ORANGE TIGER KITTEN, ADOPTED ❤ A066751, TUCKER, A NEUTERED MALE BLACK TIGER CAT, ADOPTED ❤ A066728, SKYLER, A SPAYED FEMALE TORTOISE SHELL CAT, EUTHANIZED ❤ A066737, A MALE WHITE NEW ZEALAND RABBIT WITH LIGHT BROWN EARS, EUTHANIZED ❤ A066730, BRIAR, A MALE BLACK RABBIT, BREED RESCUED ❤ A066747, A MALE WHITE RABBIT, EUTHANIZED ❤ A066760, A FEMALE WHITE RABBIT, EUTHANIZED ❤ A066761, FEMALE WHITE RABBIT, EUTHANIZED ❤ A066762, A FEMALE WHITE RABBIT, EUTHANIZED ❤ A066763, A FEMALE WHITE RABBIT, EUTHANIZED ❤ A066764, A FEMALE WHITE RABBIT, EUTHANIZED ❤ A066765, A MALE WHITE RABBIT, EUTHANIZED ❤ A065954, CHARLIE, A NEUTERED MALE DOBERMAN MIX, EUTHANIZED ❤ A066766, A FEMALE GOLDISH-BROWN AUSTRALIAN SHEPHERD/CHOW MIX, EUTHANIZED ❤ A066779, NINE WHITE ROOSTERS, EUTHANIZED ❤ A066770, PORKCHOP, A NEUTERED MALE TRICOLOR AUSTRALIAN CATTLE DOG MIX WEARING A MULTI-COLOR COLLAR, ADOPTED ❤ A066786, RIVER, A FEMALE WHITE AUSTRALIAN CATTLE DOG MIX WITH TAN ON HER FACE, BACK AND TAIL AND WEARING A PURPLE NYLON COLLAR, RECLAIMED ❤ A066769, KELLY, A SPAYED FEMALE REDDISH-BROWN GERMAN SHEPHERD MIX WITH SABLE POINTS AND WEARING A SILVER CHOKE CHAIN, EUTHANIZED ❤ A066801, MOCHA, A NEUTERED MALE BROWN AND CREAM CAT

WEARING A MULTI-COLOR NYLON COLLAR, RECLAIMED ❤ A066780, A FEMALE CHOCOLATE POINT SIAMESE MIX CAT WITH BLUE EYES AND TORTOISE SHELL POINTS, ADOPTED ❤ A066731, A MALE BLACK CAT, EUTHANIZED ❤ A066781, A FEMALE BLACK CAT WITH NO TAIL, BREED RESCUED ❤ A066778, A FEMALE CALICO KITTEN WITH A WHITE FACE AND BLACK EARS, ADOPTED ❤ A066792, A MALE ORANGE TABBY KITTEN, ADOPTED ❤ A066782, A FEMALE CHARCOAL GRAY CAT, EUTHANIZED ❤ A066772, A NEUTERED MALE BLACK CAT WITH A WHITE NOSE AND WHITE FEET, ADOPTED ❤ A066773, A FEMALE WHITE AND BLACK CAT, EUTHANIZED ❤ A066783, A MALE BROWN TIGER KITTEN, ADOPTED ❤ A066798, CABO, A MALE BROWN TIGER KITTEN, ADOPTED ❤ A066774, LINUS, A MALE BLACK AND WHITE KITTEN, ADOPTED ❤ A066773, A FEMALE WHITE AND BLACK CAT, EUTHANIZED ❤ A066795, TANGERINE, A FEMALE ORANGE AND WHITE CAT, ADOPTED ❤ A066797, A LITTER OF FIVE BUFF COLORED KITTENS, EUTHANIZED ❤ A066796, PUMPKIN PIE, A FEMALE ORANGE TIGER KITTEN, ADOPTED ❤ A066771, JACK, A MALE BROWN TIGER SCOTTISH FOLD KITTEN, ADOPTED ❤ A066815, MAMAS, A FEMALE CALICO CAT, EUTHANIZED AT GUARDIAN'S REQUEST ❤ A005657, MIEL, A NEUTERED MALE YELLOW LABRADOR RETRIEVER, RECLAIMED ❤ A066806, A FEMALE GREY AND WHITE RABBIT, BREED RESCUED ❤ A066805, A MALE WHITE NEW ZEALAND RABBIT, BREED RESCUED ❤ A066807, GARFIELD, A NEUTERED MALE BUFF TIGER CAT WITH WHITE ON HIS CHEST AND FEET, ADOPTED ❤ A066816, A FEMALE GRAY TIGER KITTEN, ADOPTED ❤ A066822, A MALE BROWN TIGER KITTEN, ADOPTED ❤ A066819, SHELLY, A FEMALE PASTEL TORTOISE SHELL KITTEN, ADOPTED ❤ A066818, A FEMALE BLACK CAT WITH WHITE ON HER CHEST, EUTHANIZED ❤ A066820, A FEMALE BLACK AND WHITE KITTEN, ADOPTED ❤ A066811, A MALE BLACK CAT WITH A WHITE SPOT ON HIS CHEST, EUTHANIZED ❤ A066813, A FEMALE SEAL POINT BIRMAN CAT WITH CLIPPED FUR ON BODY AND TAIL AND BLUE EYES, EUTHANIZED ❤ A066814, WILLOW, A SPAYED FEMALE BROWN SEAL POINT CAT, BREED RESCUED ❤ A066804, AN EVISCERATED DOG, NO OTHER DESCRIPTION, DEAD ON ARRIVAL ❤ A066929, A TAN CAT WITH BROWN POINTS, SEX UNKNOWN, DEAD ON ARRIVAL ❤ A066829, A NEUTERED MALE BROWN TIGERCAT WITH WHITE ON HIS CHEST, LEGS AND FEET, DEAD ON ARRIVAL ❤ A066832, A GRAY INJURED POSSUM, EUTHANIZED ❤ A066834, CASEY, A FEMALE GREY AND WHITE CAT, EUTHANIZED AT GUARDIAN'S REQUEST ❤ A066830, AN INJURED MALE ORANGE AND WHITE CAT, RECLAIMED AT VETERINARIAN ❤ A067805, A FEMALE BROWN TABBY KITTEN WITH WHITE TICKING, ADOPTED ❤ A067907, GRACIE, A FEMALE GRAY TIGER KITTEN, ADOPTED ❤ A067806, A MALE BUFF TABBY KITTEN WITH WHITE MARKINGS, ADOPTED ❤ A066841, A MALE ORANGE TABBY KITTEN, ADOPTED ❤ A066831, MERLIN, A MALE BLACK KITTEN, ADOPTED ❤ A066840, A BROWN TIGER KITTEN, SEX UNKNOWN, EUTHANIZED ❤ A066835, A FEMALE BROWN TIGER KITTEN, EUTHANIZED ❤ A066853, A BLACK AND WHITE SKUNK, DEAD ON ARRIVAL ❤ A066864, PEPSI, A NEUTERED MALE BLACK AND WHITE BORDER COLLIE WEARING A BLUE NYLON COLLAR, RECLAIMED ❤ A066860, CAMPBELL SOUP, A MALE ORANGE CAT WEARING A PINK AND PURPLE FLEA COLLAR, ADOPTED ❤ A066863, A NEUTERED MALE BUFF TIGER CAT, EUTHANIZED ❤ A066866, A MALE WHITE KITTEN WITH ONE BLUE EYE AND ONE YELLOW EYE, ADOPTED ❤ A064940, A FEMALE BLACK AND WHITE BORDER COLLIE MIX WITH PUPPIES, ADOPTED ❤ A066875, JESSE, A FEMALE BLACK BORDER COLLIE MIX PUPPY WITH WHITE LEGS, BELLY, AND WHITE MARKS ON HEAD, ADOPTED ❤ A067962, A MALE BLACK BORDER COLLIE MIX PUPPY WITH A WHITE BLAZE ON HIS CHEST AND WHITE ON HIS PAWS, ADOPTED ❤ A067959, PENNY, A FEMALE BLACK BORDER COLLIE MIX PUPPY WITH SOME WHITE ON HER PAWS, ADOPTED ❤ A067961, CLEA, A FEMALE BLACK BORDER COLLIE MIX PUPPY WITH A TINY AMOUNT OF WHITE ON HER PAWS, ADOPTED ❤ A067963, A MALE BLACK BORDER COLLIE MIX PUPPY WITH SOME WHITE ON HIS PAWS, ADOPTED ❤ A066865, MIDNIGHT, A FEMALE BLACK BABY RABBIT WITH FLOPPY EARS, BREED RESCUED ❤ A066867, COSMO, A MALE GRAY AND WHITE KITTEN, ADOPTED ❤ A066856, MAN-DO, A FEMALE BLACK KITTEN WITH TIGER STRIPES ON HER LEGS AND FEET, ADOPTED ❤ A066871, ANNABELLE, A FEMALE TORTOISE SHELL KITTEN, BREED RESCUED ❤ A066872, DANIEL, A MALE SEAL POINT KITTEN, ADOPTED ❤ A066857, A FEMALE BLACK SMOKE TIGER KITTEN, TRANSFERRED TO ANOTHER SHELTER ❤ A066869, PRINCESS, A FEMALE BLACK AND WHITE CAT KITTEN, ADOPTED ❤ A066870, A FEMALE SEAL POINT KITTEN, ADOPTED ❤ A066890, COOKIE, A FEMALE WHITE AND BLACK RABBIT, BROUGHT IN DEAD BY HER GUARDIAN ❤ A066877, A MALE GREY TIGER KITTEN, EUTHANIZED ❤ A060296, KENDALL, A SPAYED FEMALE BRINDLE STAFFORDSHIRE TERRIER WITH A WHITE CHEST AND WEARING A RED COLLAR WITH WHITE HEARTS, RECLAIMED ❤ A066878, A MALE BLACK AND TAN SHEPHERD MIX WEARING A RED NYLON COLLAR AND CHOKE CHAIN, EUTHANIZED ❤ A066876, TYSON, A MALE BLACK ROTTWEILER MIX, ADOPTED ❤ A062943, JENNY, A FEMALE BLACK AND TAN DOBERMAN MIX, EUTHANIZED ❤ A066874, BASIL, A BLACK RABBIT, ADOPTED ❤ A066894, A WHITE NEWBORN KITTEN, SEX UNKNOWN, EUTHANIZED ❤ A068269, A FEMALE BLACK MANX MIX KITTEN, DIED AT FOSTER HOME ❤ A067260, SCRAPPY, A FEMALE BLACK MANX MIX KITTEN, ADOPTED ❤

THANK YOU...

To Kathy Ninneman, Laura Martin, Monique Leduc, JP Novic
and The Center for Animal Protection and Education,
for their immeasurable help, support, and encouragement.

To Windi Wojdak, Andrea Lee, Deborah "OT" Tucker, Devon Eilers,
for their incredible courage and honesty.

To Laura Moretti, Ed Duvin, Kenneth White, Steve Grunow, Craig Brestrup, Bob Christensen,
for their writings that helped sow the seeds of this book.

To Rod Coronado, John Trudell, Derrick Jensen, Tom Campbell, James Nachtwey,
and all the activists and artists who use their lives and work to make a better world,
for inspiration, guidance, and hope.

To Sajid Martin,
for bringing this book to life.

To Mike Miller,
for the splendid design of this book.

To Mary Sweeley Castro,
for perspective and heart that shaped this book's voice.

To Helen Jones,
for teaching a life of compassion and joy.

To Bob Geyer,
for his unshakable support,
and for always having room in his heart and home for one more.

To Kevin,
for unflinching truth and honesty, despite the cost.

To the animals who have graced our lives, the animals we know, and the ones we don't,
the animals in our homes, and the ones in our shelters,
the animals here, and the ones yet to come.

And to shelter workers everywhere, who bear the burden, the pain, the guilt, and the grief...
we send you courage, clarity of vision, passion, and hope.

ALL OUR RELATIONS.

This book was made possible with the support of:
Devon Eilers, The J.G. & P.S. Palmer Foundation, Nell Cliff/Porter Sesnon Foundation,
Lynda Watson, Cherie Maitland/Our Furry Friends, Margaret Rinner & Lynne Acterberg/Project Purr,
The Guacamole Fund, Joan DeNeffe, Carmel Granger, JP Novic, Jody Cramer, Robert & Kathleen
Ninneman, Donna Herbst, Meryl Lewin, Rena Cochlin, Carlos Rebollar, Tracy Ely, Sam Burkhardt,
Deborah Nutcher, Kenneth Wigdal, Michelle Raffin, Lisa Lewis, Benjamin Lewis, Robyn Nayyar, Gloria
Lorenzo, Terrel & Nancy Eaton, Phil Kaplan, Kit Salisbury, Bob Geyer, Rich Apple, Judy Cassada,
Violet French, Al French, Paula Ash & Dave Canino, The Center for Animal Protection and Education.